OUTRAGEOUS
Grace

Finding a
Forever Friendship
With God

DWIGHT K. NELSON

Pacific Press® Publishing Association
Nampa, Idaho
Oshawa, Ontario, Canada

Edited by Kenneth R. Wade
Designed by Michelle Petz

Copyright 1998 by
Pacific Press® Publishing Association
Printed in the United States of America
All Rights Reserved

ISBN 0-8163-1679-1

98 99 00 01 02 • 5 4 3 2 1

Dedication

To Kirk and Kristin

Acknowledgments

In his book *What's So Amazing About Grace?* Philip Yancey observes that reading a list of names on someone's acknowledgment page is a lot like listening to the acceptance speeches at the Academy Awards, "when actors and actresses thank everyone from their kindergarten nannies to their third-grade piano teachers." Well, my third-grade piano teacher was my mother—and, of course, I'm deeply grateful for her—and my father too!

But beyond that and them, I want to acknowledge that this manuscript was birthed out of a long, shared journey with a community of people—young and old—I've been privileged to call family and home now for fifteen years. (Which in itself has been a gift of "outrageous grace!") It was at the Pioneer Memorial Church on the campus of Andrews University that these pictures of God were first sketched and painted on the canvas of our worship together week after week after week. Truly blessed is the pastor whose parish is a place of lively dialogue and thoughtful study about God. I am thankful!

But sermon notes are one matter—a book manuscript quite another. Which is why I'm grateful for Ken Wade, whose professional skills as a book editor truly went the second mile, when he not only read all my notes but listened to all the tapes of those sermons! More "outrageous grace!" Thank you for your grace with the deadlines too.

In the end, though, I wish to gratefully acknowledge the Father who gave to my wife Karen and me two wonderful children—one a "GenXer" and the other not far behind. It's out of *their* shared journey that I am learning—slowly and haltingly at times—the truth about the

Father's character of relentless love and outrageous grace. I suppose it was His plan from the beginning that children would be the clearest, widest window to His Father's heart. So to my children I dedicate this book about Him.

Dwight K. Nelson
Berrien Springs, Michigan
Easter, 1998

Chapter 1

The Death of Dag Hammarskjold and the Truth About God

What are you supposed to do, when nobody believes you? Poor Wade Miller! All he wanted was a pair of Olympic volleyball tickets. But when he called in to the Atlanta-based Olympic ticket office and placed his order, the agent on the other end of the phone didn't believe his story. Because when Miller gave her his address in Santa Fe, New Mexico, she put him on hold, then came back and announced to him that she couldn't sell tickets to somebody living outside of the United States.

"Outside of the United States? I'm in New Mexico."

"I'm sorry, sir. You'll need to contact your own national committee in Mexico."

"But I don't live in Mexico! I'm here in *New* Mexico."

"I'm awfully sorry, sir, but you'll have to call your nation's Olympic committee."

For the next thirty minutes on that long-distance phone call, Wade Miller tried to prove to the Olympic agent that New Mexico was a part of the United States. But all to no avail. He later recounted, "I asked them, 'You've never heard of Los Alamos, where they did all the atomic testing?' It's right next to Arizona. Underneath Colorado, next to Texas and Oklahoma, there is a state called New Mexico." Miller kept trying, "We have a big city called Albuquerque." Again, to no avail.

Finally the agent's supervisor got on the line. And in a classic rejoinder, she told Miller, "Sir, New Mexico, old Mexico, it doesn't matter. I understand it's a territory, but you still have to go through your nation's Olympic committee." Only when Miller gave them a Phoenix, Arizona, address did they issue him the tickets!

What are you supposed to do when nobody believes you?

What if you're God? And still nobody believes you? What's a God to do? Because even when they do believe, how many of them, how many of us, still believe the lie?

The truth is that most of the world is the victim of that lie—I know I've fallen for it more than once—a lie of such cosmic dimensions that its cosmic consequences now affect every human being on this planet!

What lie? you ask. The lie that was birthed on that glorious primeval morning, when like a shaft of gold the morning sunlight streamed through the emerald patchwork ceiling of a sprawling orchard garden. The early morning dew still clinging to the fruit-laden boughs transformed that garden into a shimmering acre of diamonds. She stepped into the acre and stepped up to the tree. She heard the voice.

"Pssst. Up here," it seemed to whisper. The woman slowly raised her gaze into the verdant foliage, higher and higher, until finally their eyes met, the eyes of the first woman and the eyes of the first serpent, a resplendent coiled serpent that for that moment of the primordial morning was but a medium or channel for the fallen rebel angel. Eve and Lucifer at a tree in a garden called Eden. Here it was that the lie was birthed in the beginning.

" 'Did God say, "You shall not eat from any tree in the garden"?' " (Genesis 3:1 NRSV—unless otherwise noted all scriptural quotations will be from the New Revised Standard Version). The crafty serpent's innocent banter was only a front for the slick modus operandus of deception that has worked for him ever since the beginning. And that is, simply engage your victim in conversation, set up a debate, get her, get him to talk back. It worked with Eve, and it's worked ever since with all of us. Because talking back to the devil and arguing with the serpent is a sure-fire formula for defeat! Don't even answer him when you hear his "pssst!"

But Eve did. Because he tricked her into a debate with an absolute fabrication! Had God forbidden Adam and Eve from eating from *any* tree in Eden? Of course not! In fact God had told them the very opposite—He told them they could eat of every tree in the garden *except* for one. God is love. And Love never forces itself on anyone, even His very first children. Which is why God put a tree in the middle of the garden that became the place where Adam and Eve could go *if* they chose to reject God's love and follow Lucifer's lie. "But please, stay away from that tree. All it can bring you is death." Divine love, human love, no love can be love unless it offers the one it loves the right to say No to that love. And so God gave them the choice. Hence the tree in the middle of the garden.

But Lucifer, in the guise of that shimmering serpent, completely fogs over the issue of freedom of choice, and instead garbs God in the haughty garment of selfish denial. "God simply doesn't want you to enjoy something good" is what he implied in his deceptive question.

"Oh, no," Eve shot back. "We can eat of any trees in Eden. It's just this one God has forbidden."

"Phooey," the serpent hissed back. "God is just afraid that if you eat this fruit, you'll become like Him. Why look at me! I ate it, and I can talk. You eat it, and you shall be as God Himself!" (See verses 2-5.)

Mean, old, stingy God. The insinuation is now all in

place: How could you ever love Somebody so cruel as to leave something that good out of your reach? And if you cannot love Him, then how could you ever trust Him? And if you can't trust Him, then surely He is Someone to be afraid of!

There it was, there it is. The lie that trickled off the forked tongue of the serpent deceiver. A baldfaced lie that has been respun and rewoven a billion trillion times since. The lie: *God is someone to be afraid of.*

Running from God

The lie that began with a question worked like a charm, a very hypnotic charm. And Adam and Eve swallowed it hook, line, and sinker. For in the very next words of Genesis 3 there is that unforgettable, heartbreaking moment. God has come down for an evening stroll with His two favorite earthling children. But alas, they are nowhere to be found. The Creator calls out into the twilight shadows, "Where are you?" but no answer. Strange. Where are they? Then God spots a moving bush, but He hadn't created a trembling bush. And so God calls out to Adam, who with Eve is hiding behind the shadowy cover. With trembling lips Adam and Eve emerge, and it is Adam who speaks: " 'I heard the sound of you in the garden, *and I was afraid'* " (Genesis 3:10).

There it is in all its naked shame. The lie of Lucifer: *God is someone to be afraid of.* The lie Adam and Eve fell for and an entire human race has fallen for ever since.

You think about it. This lie permeates every world religion. I was born in Japan and grew up in Asia. I have seen the lie acted out in the fearful formalities of Buddhism, Hinduism, and Shintoism. Etched deep within the worshipers' motionless features is a numinous fear that inspires such meticulous motions of worship born of the desperate human longing to appease a wrathful, vengeful God. The instructions are the same the world over: read the Book (and every religion has one), follow the directions, obey the commands, and hope to God you're saved in the end. Like a mantra the instructions keep repeating themselves: read the Book, follow the direction, and hope you're saved.

God is someone to be afraid of. The lie permeates Islam as well. And Judaism. And sadly enough it has penetrated all too much of Christianity too. Because the father of all lies, the father of all fear, the primeval deceiver Satan has fingered even the Bible itself and turned it into a tale of terror in the minds of too many.

I know people who have actually gone through the Scriptures and counted how many times God punished people therein—as if by assembling all such stories one could paint an accurate portrait of God. Some say there are over sixty stories where God is depicted as being the One who punishes and destroys people.

With devilish glee Satan has warped God's testament of love into a testimony of fear. And as his hellish starting point, he keeps hissing the lie: God is someone to be afraid of. "I told you so," he taunts. "Better be afraid of Him, because if you cross God, look what happens!"

And so people in every culture and every religion have learned to be afraid of God, to run from Him, to appease Him with the desperate hope that He won't strike them with pain or suffering or tragedy. All because they have believed the lie.

Punishment and love

But those who say that the Bible portrays God as Someone we should be afraid of are ignoring one crucial piece of evidence—a critical piece in the mosaic that forms the portrait of God. It is a compelling text with a truth that belies the lie and unravels the deception. It's found in the book of Hebrews, in chapter 12, which comes immediately after the chapter known as the Bible Hall of Fame, Hall of Faith chapter. Hebrews 11 reviews the history of the followers of God, and chapter 12 draws the lessons from that history. And here we find the crucial lesson we must not ignore: "And you have forgotten [and how easy it is for us to forget] the exhortation that addresses you as children— 'My child, do not regard lightly the discipline of the Lord, or lose heart when you are punished by him; for the Lord disciplines those whom he loves, and chastises every child whom he accepts' " (Hebrews 12:5,6).

We have misread the Old Testament, because we have used a lie to interpret the truth. Because we have ignored this very important reality: The stories of divine punishment are the stories of divine *love!*

Why, I suppose nearly every parent knows the meaning of that truth. Karen and I have been blessed with two wonderful children, Kirk and Kristin. When our kids were much younger, it was necessary for me to explain to them the dangers of the neighborhood road out in front of our home. I'd get down to their eye level and carefully outline the reasons why we were making the road off limits for them and their play. "Daddy doesn't want you to go out into the road, please. Because a big car could come around the corner and go BOOM and hit you and hurt you and that would be terrible. OK?" And of course, they both would nod in agreement.

But for the sake of illustration, let's say I look out a few minutes later and see Kirk playing in the middle of the forbidden street. What's a father to do? Of course, being a dad, I hurry out across the yard and into the street where my son is, I take him by the hand, march him back into the yard, get back down to eye-level, and (being a father of grace and love) re-explain my reasons for Kirk's not playing in the street. "Do you understand me?" And he obediently nods.

Now, if I look out the window a few minutes later and see my son back in the middle of the road playing, what do I do now? The same routine as before, only with much more vigor and a brand new ending! Because I love my boy and want to protect him from danger and death, I will impress that love upon him, by warming a certain portion of his anatomy (namely his gluteous maximus) so that the truth will be red hot in another portion of his anatomy (namely his mind)!

"'My child, do not regard lightly the discipline of the Lord, . . . for the Lord disciplines those whom he loves.' " Every parent knows that if you really love your child, punishment and discipline are an integral part of demonstrating that saving love.

One author describes God's methodology in some of the Old Testament stories as God's "fire rescue method." Because if a building is burning down, every fireman knows you don't have time to casually talk or slowly reason through your rescue methods with the victims trapped on the third floor of the inferno. When the building is going up in flame and smoke, you have only one option with the victims. Grab and drag to safety immediately. If they're screaming in panic, even more drastic action is mandated. With your hand over the mouth and your arm over the flailing limbs, grab and drag to safety immediately. There will be time enough later to explain it to them. Extricate now. Explain later.

And so God did throughout the Old Testament. Many were the times when God had to hurriedly grab people and drag them kicking and screaming to safety. Times when He had to say "I'll explain it later."

The explanation

And when He did explain it later, it was the most glorious explanation the universe had ever or has ever witnessed.

A powerful hint of God's explanation came wrapped up in the miracle story of John the Baptist's birth. Old man Zechariah was a priest and it was his turn for the temple duties. While he was officiating in the inner sanctum of the Jerusalem temple, suddenly a tall shining angel materializes in front of his astonished eyes with the incredible announcement that he and his wife Elizabeth are going to have a baby boy. But that's impossible, the elderly priest shoots back. Do you realize how old we are? It was then that a supernatural sign was "imposed" upon the disbelieving Zechariah, "'But now, because you did not believe my words, . . . you will become mute, unable to speak, until the day these things occur'" (Luke 1:20). And so it is that his wife becomes pregnant and enjoys nine months of peace and quiet.

Until the miracle baby is born and Zechariah's tongue is miraculously loosed. And when he can talk again, the elderly new father sings a most beautiful paean of praise, an anthem about the coming Messiah. And in one stanza resounds the incredible truth, " 'that we, being rescued from the hands of our enemies, might serve him [the soon-coming Saviour] *without fear*'" (Luke 1:74).

There it is, the glorious explanation that God promised through the ages. The Saviour will come, and when He does you will worship Him *without fear!* Jesus the Saviour would come to tell the truth about God, to put the lie to the lie—to reveal to the human race and to the universe that the story spun by the father of all lies was itself a lie. God is *not* someone to be afraid of! You don't have to be afraid of God at all.

And so He came, the Messiah, the Saviour of the world, Jesus of Nazareth. Another miracle Baby who would be called Immanuel, "God is with us." And when the Baby of Bethlehem grew up to become the Man of Galilee, over and over Jesus would keep repeating the promise, " 'If you know me, you will know my Father also. . . . Whoever has seen me has seen the Father. . . . I am in the Father and the Father is in me'" (John 14:7, 9, 11). " 'Come to me. . . . and learn from me; for I am gentle and humble in heart'" (Matthew 11:28, 29). " 'Anyone who comes to me I will never drive away' " (John 6:37).

And she did come to Him, a ravaged young prostitute. Oh, it's true, she didn't come on her own—she was tossed in a heap at Jesus' feet. But the story in John 8 chronicles what happens when you come to this God.

They had caught her in the act, in bed with a man who wasn't her husband. Now the ecclesiastical leaders had the perfect trap with which to bring down the popular young Teacher from Nazareth. Throwing the disheveled woman at Jesus' sandals one morning in the temple, before the gawking crowd the prelates loudly demanded to know what Jesus recommended as her punishment. After all, the law of Moses commanded the adulteress be stoned to death. (Which was only half the truth, since the same law commanded the same sentence for both adulterous parties.)

Smugly the ecclesiastics await Jesus' reply. For if He says, "Don't stone her," the elders will turn to the crowd and crow, "Did we not tell you He was a lawbreaker?" But if He decides, "Stone her," then the clerics will hurry off to the Roman governor and decry this man who would take Rome's prerogative of capital punishment into his own hands. Damned if He did and damned if He didn't, it was the perfect trap.

But Jesus doesn't answer. He quietly kneels to the dusty temple floor and begins to write with His finger in the dust. A well-known tradition has taught that what Jesus wrote in the dust were the secret sins of the elders who accused the young woman. What a portrait of God! Only twice in the Scriptures is He Himself shown as writing with His finger. Once when He wrote the Eternal Law on two tables of stone. And once when He wrote the sins of the leaders in the dust of the floor. On stone so that time could not erase the truth of His Ten Commandments. But in the dust so that one puff of breeze would erase the record of their private sins. Jesus wouldn't embarrass even His enemies. What grace, what love, what a God!

And when He was through writing in the temple dust, Jesus stood back up with the quiet command, "'Let anyone among you who is without sin be the first to throw a stone at her'" (John 8:7). And the story reads that one by one the prelates quietly slipped away, their angry accusations silenced. Lifting her head to meet His eyes, Jesus gazes into her tear-stained, mascara-streaked face and asks, "Woman, where are your accusers? Has no one condemned you?" She haltingly shakes her head. They are all gone, her accusers. Then the incarnate God speaks, "'Neither do I condemn you. Go your way, and from now on do not sin again'" (John 8:11).

What Jesus demonstrated that sunlit day in the story of John 8, He also taught on that moonlit night in the story of John 3. It must be included, this piece in the mosaic portrait of God that we are piecing together here. How beloved and well-known is John 3:16—"'For God so loved the world that he gave his only Son, so that everyone who believes in him may not perish but may have eternal life.'" But we ought to memorize verse 17 also: "'Indeed, God did not send the Son into the world to condemn the world, but in order that the world might be saved through him.'"

Not someone to be afraid of

"You've had it all wrong," the Son of God said. "You have believed a lie about God. God is not someone to be afraid of. I have not come to condemn you. I have come to love you— to save you—by demonstrating to you the eternal truth about God: You don't have to be afraid of Him."

Even if you don't want Him. Even if in the end you turn your back on Him and walk away from Him and say that you want nothing at all to do with Him. Even then, God is still not someone to be afraid of. This breathtaking truth emerged in all its dramatic glory on that treacherous night before Jesus died.

The angry, bobbing orange torches stab cruelly into the silver night of another Passover moon. Like a pack of fireflies the torches hurriedly wind and wend their way up the rocky pathway to the hillside garden. Coarse voices break the midnight still that moments ago muffled the sobs of the God-man who weeps over the tragic consequences of sin. But Jesus' tears are dried now. He stands alone in the dark to meet His betrayer.

I don't know if you've ever been betrayed by someone very close to you, some you loved and trusted deeply. If you have, you remember the pain. The cutting, stabbing pain that begins in your stomach. And moves into your throat. A pain you cannot cry away. A pain that will not go away.

Jesus stands alone in the night and stares into the eerily orange face of His betrayer. And as He looks into the face of Judas, what do you suppose is going through the mind of God? Jesus has always known the heart of Judas. From the beginning when Judas pushed his executive skills upon the fledgling band of disciples. Do you suppose that it was kept a secret from Jesus who it was who was pilfering the meager treasury, the shared money purse that the disciples kept among them? Of course the Master knows who has been embezzling the funds. It is Judas. But never does Jesus embarrass Judas in public. He tells a parable once upon a time that nails Judas as guilty, but no one but Judas recognizes the parable's throbbing point.

Oh yes, Jesus knows Judas. And divine love keeps pleading with that guilty heart. Why earlier this very night, the Saviour had bent down and washed the feet of His betrayer. But Judas exercised his inalienable right to say No to God, and he did. And now it is night. A very dark night.

Jesus stands in the Garden of Gethsemane as that steely cold heart—one that would not respond even to the greatest love in the universe—steps out of the shadows and walks toward Him. His arms outstretched, feigning affection, Judas plants a noisy kiss on the cheek of his Master. Held in the embrace of His betrayer, what do you suppose Jesus calls him now? "You dirty, lost, hellbent sinner, get away from Me!"—was that the response of the Saviour? Oh no. Jesus has a single, simple word for the one who betrays Him. He calls him *friend*. Read the astounding evidence for yourself in Matthew 26:50—"Friend, do what you are here to do." Can you believe it? God looks into the face of His betrayer and calls him "Friend."

Never forget that picture of God, my friend. It is worth more than ten thousand words and that many books! When Jesus calls Judas His friend, we see the truth at last: *God is not someone to be afraid of—He is someone to be a friend of!*

That very same night, a few hours later, Peter discovers the same truth at that moment when he reaches into his fisherman's book of obscenities and turns the chilled night air blue with oaths, "I never knew that blankety-blank-blank-blank Man in my life!" Nobody would now mistake him for being a follower and friend of this condemned Jesus of Nazareth. But no sooner had the obscenities left his lips than a rooster was heard crowing the coming of dawn, and instantly Peter remembered Jesus' prediction that he would deny his Lord three times. Peter whirls around to see if Jesus might have heard his swearing denial. Luke describes the heartbreaking moment: "The Lord turned and looked at Peter" (Luke 22:61). And Jesus' eyes whispered to Peter what He had spoken to Judas, "Friend."

Same Jesus. Same word *friend*. Judas hears it, and because he has grown up with the lie that God is somebody to be afraid of, he goes out and takes his own life. Peter hears it, and because Peter has learned that God is not someone to be afraid of but someone to be a friend of, Peter does not take his life. He goes out, broken-hearted, and *finds* his life.

If only Judas had found the same truth, he would have found the same forgiveness as Peter. Denier, betrayer, sinner—it doesn't matter with God. For His is a grace that is outrageous. More outrageous than the serpent's lie!

"There is no fear in love, but perfect love casts out fear" (1 John 4:18). Because perfect Love isn't Somebody to be afraid of—perfect Love is Somebody to be a friend of.

And that is the plain and simple gospel truth about God. Not Someone to be afraid of, Jesus' outstretched arms on Calvary proclaim the incontrovertible truth: God is Someone to be a friend of.

Not afraid, but a friend. It's the difference between life and death.

The death of Dag Hammarskjold

You may be wondering what all this could possibly have to do with the death of Dag Hammarskjold. If you don't remember him, he was the Secretary General of the United Nations from 1953 through 1961. A Swedish Christian, he wrote the celebrated collection of spiritual meditations, *Markings*. Many regard him as the greatest diplomat in the twentieth century and, without doubt, the greatest secretary general in the beleaguered history of the United Nations. He died in a tragic plane crash in the Congo in 1961, and was posthumously awarded the Nobel Peace Prize.

The circumstances surrounding his death remained a mystery long afterward. Hammarskjold was in the strife-torn Congo on a peace mission to the warring factions. Sometime in the night between September 17 and 18, the plane in which the Secretary General was flying went down in Zambia in a fiery explosion.

The cause of the accident remained a mystery, until the investigators discovered a new clue as they continued to sift through the evidence. Someone noticed that in the cockpit of the wreckage there was an open map to Ndolo, which is the name of the airport in Leopoldville (now Kinshasa), Congo. Evidently on that fateful night the pilot had been studying the charts for Ndolo airport. Which would have been fine, except for the fact that their intended flight destination that night was a city called Ndola in Zambia.

Looking at the map for Ndolo instead of Ndola, the pilot mistakenly thought he had a thousand more feet before he would land at the Ndola airstrip. But he was looking at the wrong map. And so, suddenly, without warning, in the pitch-blackness of that night, the plane plowed into the ground when the pilot thought he still had a thousand feet to descend.

Ndolo. Ndola. The only difference in those names is a single letter. And yet the difference between an *a* and an *o* was the difference between life and death.

Afraid or *a friend.* Just the difference of a few letters. But when it comes to the map of God, it, too, is the difference between life and death.

So which map are you following? Is God someone to be *afraid* of, or someone to be *a friend* of? In the pages ahead I invite you to sift through the evidence with me. Because it is imperative we find the right map. Not according to the death of Dag Hammerskjold, but according to the life and death of Jesus Christ. For His is the only death that belies the lie and restores the truth—*God is not somebody to be afraid of, He is someone to be a friend of.*

Isn't it time we abandoned the lie and embraced the Life?

Chapter 2

On Playing Marbles
With God

The children in the church school had been learning the Ten Commandments, and now it was time to review the commandments and discover how well they had mastered the material. Rather than call for rote memory repetition, the teacher decided to use "case studies" to ascertain her students' ability to apply the Decalogue.

"Boys and girls," she said, "Junior and Sissie were brother and sister. One evening Junior's parents came to him and said, 'We're taking Sissie to town with us. Would you please do the dishes. And please don't watch any television until the dishes are done.' Junior agreed, but when his parents and sister came home later that evening, they found him watching TV, and the dishes weren't done! Now, children, which commandment does that story illustrate?"

A bright young scholar instantly waved his hand, "I know, Teacher. 'Honor thy father and thy mother.'"

"Very good, Billy. Now here's another story. When Sissie and her parents were in town that evening, they passed by a store counter with delicious candies spread out on top. And Sissie sneaked out her hand and grabbed a piece of candy. Now, which commandment does that illustrate?"

Another hand shot up and a youthful voice blurted out, "I know that one, Teacher. 'Thou shalt not steal.'"

"Very good, Marie! You children are doing well!"

But now came a more difficult case study. How do you illustrate to children the tenth commandment, "Thou shalt not covet"? But the teacher had a story ready.

"Junior and Sissie both collect stamps. And one day Sissie had her stamp albums spread open on her bed. Junior passed by the room and stopped to examine her stamps and noticed a stamp she had that he didn't have. 'I want that stamp, Sissie!' he exclaimed.

"'No, you can't have that one—it's the only one I've got,' she replied.

"'But I want that stamp!'

"And again, 'No, you can't have it.'

"Well, finally, boys and girls, Junior stomped out of the room. Soon he returned with their pet cat in his hands. With one hand he held the cat and with the other he held the cat's tail. 'Listen here, Sissie,' he announced, 'if you don't give me that stamp, I'm going to rip this tail off!'"

The teacher had the youngsters' undivided attention. "Now, children, which commandment does that illustrate?"

The children sat in silence, their minds scrambling to figure this one out. Suddenly, little Jimmy in the back row jumped to his feet waving his hand. "I know, I know, Teacher." She nodded and so he went on, "'What God hath joined together, let no man put asunder!'"

Now there's a new commandment! I don't recall that one being among the ten, do you? But those ancient words, once upon a time spoken by Jesus about marriage, have a lot to do with the truth about God and outrageous grace. A truth that once it's joined together must never be put asunder. We must never separate our understanding of this God—who is not someone to be afraid of, but someone to be a friend of—from the picture of outrageous grace that He has revealed in the Bible. An outrageous grace that comes shining through when you play marbles with God.

Marbles with God? Seem a bit preposterous? Perhaps. But let me explain. A Jewish physician friend of mine loaned me a book that he said I must read. Written by best-selling author Rabbi Harold Kushner, just its title supplies plenty of food for thought: *When All You've Ever Wanted Isn't Enough*. It was while reading that book that I became familiar with the research and writings of the great Swiss developmental psychologist, Jean Piaget. I hurried to the library and found twenty or more of his books on the shelves. I checked out the one entitled *The Moral Judgment of the Child*. In this book he describes how a child deals with right and wrong—what is permitted and what is forbidden. His conclusions are fascinating. Piaget found a disarming way to gather his data by walking the streets of Geneva and nearby Swiss towns, approaching children playing marbles, and then asking them three questions: How old are you? How do you play marbles? and, How do you know that is the way to play?

After hundreds of such interviews Piaget arrived at a revealing conclusion: Children pass through stages in their journey through marble playing. And I began to wonder: Could these stages teach us something about how we live our lives? Particularly about how we live with (or perhaps play games with) God?

Stages of the game

Stage one is where young children see the rules of a game, and by extension all the rules they are given, as having been handed down by an "unquestionable higher authority," as Kushner rephrased it. For example, here is a portion of an actual conversation with a five-year-old Swiss boy named Fal. Can you guess who is this child's "unquestionable higher authority"?

The interviewer begins: "Long ago when people were beginning to build the town of Neuchatel [where the boy lived], did little children play at marbles the way you showed me?"

"Yes."

"Always that way?"

"Yes."

"How did you get to know the rules?"

"When I was quite little my brother showed me. My daddy showed my brother."

"And how did your daddy know?"

"My daddy just knew. No one told him."

"Am I older than your daddy?"

"No, you're young. .. .My daddy had been born when we came to Neuchatel. My daddy was born before me."

"Tell me some people older than your daddy."

"My grand-dad."

"Did he play marbles?"

"Yes."

"Then he played before your daddy."

"Yes, but not with rules."

"Tell me who was born first, your daddy or your grand-dad?"

"My Daddy was born before my grand-dad."

"Where is God?"

"In the sky."

"Is He older than your daddy?"

"Not so old." (pp 46, 47, *The Moral Judgment of the Child*)

Amazing, isn't it? And pretty obvious who in Fal's life is the "unquestionable higher authority" who has laid down the rules! Why, not even God and Grandpa are as old as Daddy! Let's call stage one the **rule** stage.

Piaget discovered, however, that children playing marbles don't remain in that first stage. As they grow older, they begin to question all those childhood rules, even as they question their childhood authorities. "Who says we have to do it this way?" And so adolescents go through an irresponsible stage where they make up their own silly rules, resulting in the game of marbles becoming either too easy or too difficult. Let's call this the **rebel** stage, where rebelling against authority is the hallmark.

But Piaget also discovered that these same youth can come to the place where they finally conclude that if they're going to make their own rules, they need to adopt fair and reasonable ones. Now, Piaget says, they are at the "threshold of maturity." Rules are no longer embraced as simply handed down from on high. Rules are concerned with "mutual respect." Rules have to do with relationships rather than authority. In this third stage, relationship transcends rule. It is the **relationship** stage.

Playing marbles with God

But what does playing marbles have to do with God? Perhaps much more than we first thought!

Could it be that Piaget's discovery about the stages children go through in their relationship to authority and rules is in fact a description of our pilgrimage through life, our quest for God? So that one of these three stages describes your way of relating to God—and mine too? Piaget himself suggests that the children's attitude toward the game of marbles is, in fact, a paradigm of our adult attitudes toward authority and rules.

After reading and musing over Piaget's conclusions for the first time, I leaned back in my chair and pondered whether the Bible confirmed these conclusions of moral psychology. Do the Holy Scriptures affirm these stages in human development? And while I wondered, I quite unexpectedly recalled an old, old story. And the more I pondered the story, the more I recognized Piaget's three stages in that story.

You know the story—the one about the farmer's young boy, who comes storming into the kitchen, the screen door slamming behind him. His young face glistens with the sweat of his afternoon chores. His eyes are angry. His voice is fed-up. "I've had it up to here," he fairly shouts at his father and mother who are seated about the red ging-ham tablecloth in the kitchen. "I'm tired of the sweat, I'm tired of the stink, tired of chickens and tired of cows! And I want out of here, Father! I'm sick and tired of this life! I've decided I'm going into investment banking, and I'm moving to New York." He finally pauses to breathe. "I'm going to find my fortune far away from this place!"

For a long lonely moment, the farmer stares up into that agitated, youthful face. Then he turns across the table and looks into the stunned eyes of his wife. No one speaks.

Finally the father slowly rises to again look his son in the eyes. "All right, Son, you may go. But . . ," and the farmer's mud-stained, callused hand reaches across and tightens on his son's shoulder, "Listen to me, Boy. If you ever want to come back, you'll always have a home here with your mother and brother and me."

Most people have heard Christ's parable of the prodigal son over and over again. But for a moment, no matter how many times you've been there before, I'd like to invite you to go back to Jesus' story and see if we can identify Piaget's three stages there—the rule stage, the rebel stage, and the relation-ship stage. And while there, perhaps we shall learn a valuable lesson about our own lives.

Where do I fit?

Remember the stage-one person—the small child—in Piaget's progression, the one who views the rules as being handed down by an unquestioned higher authority. This is the person who relates to rules as the ultimate—the final word in how to reap the rewards of the system: If you're going to get the goods, you'd better obey the rules. That's how small children naturally think. But is it any different for adults?

Is it possible that in some ways I am still a stage-one person? Or that you are? Is there a vestige of this way of thinking in the way we relate to God?

People in stage one see God as an authoritative, strict

Father, who lays down the law—the ultimate rule-giver. He is the rewarder of the obedient. He is the punisher of the disobedient. Everything with Him is Thou shalt, or Thou shalt not! God is the ultimate, unquestionable higher authority. If you want your share of the inheritance, stay in line with Him! Fall out, and you lose your piece of the pie!

Does one of the characters in Jesus' story fit into stage one?

At first you might think it's the prodigal. But think again.

I don't need to retell the whole story to you. But if you haven't heard it recently, you might want to review it in your Bible, Luke 15:11-32. But for a moment let's skip right down to the end of the story and focus in on the words of the prodigal's older brother in verses 28-30. He's come back from the field, covered with the sweat and mud and stink of a hard day's work, and he hears laughter coming from the house. What in the world is going on?! And so he calls one of the servants to him and learns that his long lost kid brother has suddenly shown up again, came home this afternoon, and now father's thrown a party to celebrate! And how does the older brother react?

"Then he became angry and refused to go in. His father came out and began to plead with him. But he answered his father, 'Listen! For all these years I have been working like a slave for you, and I have never disobeyed your command; yet you have never given me even a young goat so that I might celebrate with my friends. But when this son of yours came back, who has devoured your property with prostitutes, you killed the fatted calf for him!'" (Luke 15:28-30).

Do you hear what the older brother is saying here? "I can't figure you out, Father! Look at this. All these years I've been *slaving* for you (those are Jesus' words—*slaving for you*)! I've kept every single one of your rules—I've never disobeyed. I've never sinned grossly. I've always gone to church. I've denied myself pleasures, all because I figured

that's what you demanded of me, pleasures I would've en-
joyed now and then. But oh no! Not me, I slave for you.
And what do I get? You throw a party for this jerk of a
brother of mine, who ran away from you in the first place,
spent your fortune and slept with every woman in town,
and probably has AIDS. And me? What do I get for living
such a drab, joyless life of obedience? *Nothing!* Not a thing.
No fatted calf, no party, no nothing!"

Older brothers among us

Does the tirade of the elder brother sound at all familiar? Is it possible that you (or I) have even rehearsed that speech
a time or two in the past? Possible that there's a little corner of your heart—or maybe a very big corner—that relates
to God all on the basis of rules and regulations just as the
older brother did with his father? Could we have grown up
with a religion that has taught us to expect God's rewards
and punishments solely on the basis of our devotion to His
rules?

Rabbi Harold Kushner struggles with those questions
in his book *When Bad Things Happen to Good People.* On
page 128 he writes about people he has known who seem to
be stuck at a stage one—on the older brother level—in the
way they relate to God:

> I have known people who were deeply serious
> about their religion, people whose religious commit-
> ment was the single most powerful force in shaping
> their lives, and who nonetheless left me wondering
> whether all that religion was good for them. . . . I
> have known Jews who would spend the Sabbath not
> in serenity and spiritual refreshment, but in constant
> concern that they might be doing something forbid-
> den, until the day became a weekly ordeal to be sur-
> vived.
>
> In some cases there was a frantic obsession with
> sin, a perpetual fear that they had inadvertently bro-
> ken some rule, done something wrong and offended

God, losing their heavenly Father's love.

Sound at all familiar? Have you been playing the part of the older brother? Could it be that you and I have been following God all these years out of a sense of sullen obligation—a fearful obedience that keeps thinking, *If I don't obey Him, He's going to cut me out of His will!*

I can't help but wonder if maybe some of us are desperately playing the part of the elder brother all because we have a mistaken notion about who God is?

Don't misunderstand me, please. I'm not saying that I'm opposed to the rules and commandments of God. Of course I'm not. A loving God, like any loving parent, obviously gives protective rules and commandments. But could it be that some Christians have been following God all these years out of a sense of sullen obligation, slaving away for God because they're convinced that's the only way they'll get His inheritance?

But there's a catch-22 with such a spirit of sullen submission. Oh sure, a constant focus on rule-keeping may appear to satisfy the Ultimate Higher Authority. But number one, you're never sure. And number two, slaving away for Him brings a costly trade-off! No joy, no peace, no laughter, no freedom. No nothing but more and more of this mechanical, sullen, secretly complaining spirit of I'll-do-this-even-if-it-kills-me kind of living for God. And come on, let's be honest. Isn't that kind of sullen, joyless submission one step away from out-and-out rebellion? Sure it is! Because the someday is coming when the elder brother (or sister) wakes up to the truth and explodes in bitter frustration and rebellion. And then he, too, will run away from the Father. Oh maybe the elder sister will never be brave enough to run away on the outside, but she will nurse an angry heart that has run far away from the Father on the inside!

How could there be any peace or joy in a life like that? No wonder you can find so many stern faces in the church today. Elder brothers who've never run away, but who've really run away from the grace and love and joy and peace of the Father's house. Elder sisters, who hear the music and dancing coming from the Father's house, but refuse to go. All they know how to do is slave away for God. All because they don't know the truth about the Father.

Prodigals

Remember, though, that Piaget discovered that children typically move into a second stage of development about the time they reach adolescence. Tiring of authoritarian rules, they throw them all off and try playing the game without rules, or at least with their own set of rules and standards.

Any stage-two rebel in Jesus' parable? Of course! And he's the classic manifestation of stage two. The younger brother, the one we call the prodigal son.

Read how Jesus describes him in Luke 15:13—"'A few days later the younger son gathered all he had and traveled to a distant country, and there he squandered his property in dissolute living.'" Or as the *New International Version* puts it, "in wild living"!

What's the mindset of the stage-two rebel, the prodigal son? It more often than not is a reaction, a bold, flagrant reaction to the stage-one mentality of the elder brother. Often it goes like this: "I've had it with the conservatives, I've had it with all their authority, their restraints, their rules. I don't need anybody else telling me how to live—not my family, not my church, not my school, not my government, not anybody! Because, look at me! I'm an adult now, a free-thinking, independent grown-up human being. And besides, I'm too much a part of the Pepsi Generation NeXt— 'You've got the right one, baby, uh huh!' So I'm out of here. *Hasta la vista,* baby!'"

Once again, sound familiar? I've known many of these younger brothers and sisters, who aren't necessarily younger chronologically speaking. Many of them are very bright, very perceptive, who look at Christianity, who look at the church, and all they see is a bunch of rules. Young and not-so-young people who perceive the church, and God, as too authoritarian, too concerned with obedience rather than love. Stage-two younger brothers and sisters who've chosen to throw all of that off. To write the church off (and organized religion, for that matter), or at least to live on its fringes, looking in now and then and pitying those poor folk who are so bound and burdened by their joyless rules and regulations.

It would be funny were it not so sad. For you see, the two brothers are very much alike down deep inside. Oh it's true, the stage-two prodigals call the stage-one elder brothers conservatives. And the stage-one rules-focused elders call the stage-two rebels liberals. But beyond the name-calling, both boys really want the same thing: They want to be free. Both boys see the father as an authoritarian rule giver. Because of his rules, one boy leaves home and gets lost. Because of his rules, the other son stays home and gets lost. Both of them are wrong and both are lost, because they both have missed the real truth about the father, a stage-three truth about the father neither of them has discovered.

Relationships or rules?

And that is the truth, the real truth that when it is all said and done, *the father values relationships more than rules.*

Notice in the story that the father leaves his house, looking for *both* boys. He hurries off the front porch when in the squint of the afternoon sun he spots the distant but familiar gait of his runaway younger son stumbling back down the road toward home. Never forget that the father who races down the dusty lane with his arms outstretched to embrace and kiss the prodigal, is the same father who in the twilighted shadows of that same evening hurries out the door to welcome his elder son. Same father, same wide-open embrace, same eager and loving heart.

Why? Because the truth about the Father is the same

truth it's always been throughout eternity—what matters most to God in the beginning and in the end is *relationship*. The father doesn't hurry out of the house to restore the broken rules, his heart races toward his boys in order to restore a broken relationship. Because *the father values relationship more than rules*.

You see the truth keeps fitting. God isn't somebody to be afraid of, He's someone to be a friend of. For that very reason the Father values relationships more than rules. Of course there are rules. Every relationship in life is protected by very necessary rules. But God's preoccupation isn't with the rules; it's with the relationships.

And so it should be with the children of God, wouldn't you say? There isn't a church on earth whose primary mission is to restore the rules. But I can't imagine a church on earth, if it is a church that follows the Father, that hasn't been given the passionate mission to restore relationships.

After all, isn't that what the outstretched arms of Calvary are all about? The wide-open embrace of the Father and the Son to every runaway rebel, to every rule-driven elder: Come home to the truth about Me—I am not Someone to be afraid of, I am Someone to be a friend of, for I value relationships more than rules.

Think of the freedom of the friendship in that wide-open embrace! To fall in love with this God who will take your rebel heart back, no questions asked about your guilty, sullied past and your profligate, shameful waste, because all that matters is that you've come home to Him. To fall in love with this God whose arms are outstretched to your sullen, rules-driven heart, with the quiet assurance that all He owns has always been yours all along. So won't you abandon your slaving and embrace His friendship and step into the welcome glow of His love and joy and peace and laughter and hope once more? Oh the freedom of the friendship in that wide-open embrace!

Which, if I may repeat myself, is precisely the mission of the Christian church today. It is this picture of the Father that a relationally starved world is longing to see and know. It is this portrait of the Father that is the passionate heart and soul of everything Jesus taught and everything the Bible stands for. This is the truth about Himself God has literally been *dying* to share with this runaway planet. If only the world could see those wide-open arms of His, don't you think they'd come home? Then why don't we tell them?

A photograph of the wide-open arms

Do you remember the award-winning black and white news photograph the day the first prisoners-of-war came back from Vietnam? It was 1973. An armistice had been signed. And North Vietnam was releasing its American POWs. The giant C-140 Hercules transport landed at some West Coast air force base. The gray plane taxied off the runway onto the unloading area, and the stairway at the back of the plane was lowered to the ground. And here they came, the first returning prisoners-of-war, one by one down the stairway and across the tarmac to the cordoned-off welcoming crowd of families and lovers and friends.

But our eyes were drawn to one soldier in particular. Dressed in his crisp military khaki, his pleated cap in perfect place atop a face that was gaunt but proud. The soldier had come home.

And somebody in that crowd of well-wishers could no longer wait for her daddy to cross the tarmac. Because as the soldier father stepped off the lowered stairs, his little girl broke out of the roped-off crowd. A look of joyful ecstasy was on her face, her long dark hair streaming behind her in the airport wind, the girl raced across the tarmac. The father must have heard her call to him. Because he had spotted her. Instinctively he dropped his duffel bag to the runway and bending at his knees he threw wide his arms to catch his flying little girl. When the camera shutter snapped, her feet were off the ground, her arms in midair reaching toward her father. Click. A black-and-white moment of timelessness, the portrait of a father-and-child reunion.

So that we would never forget them, Jesus told a story once upon a time about the wide-open arms of "our Father, who art in heaven." Arms wide open with the glad and glorious truth that what has always mattered most to God is younger brothers and elder sisters stepping into His wide-open embrace.

For the life of you and the life of me, I can't think of a reason not to. Can you?

Chapter 3

A Three-letter Poison, A Four-word Appeal

I've kept an issue of *Time* Magazine in my files for nearly twenty years now. It's the December 4, 1978, issue. On the cover is the picture that sent chills up and down the spines of all who first saw its devastating full-color horror. The cover headline reads "The Cult of Death." In the foreground of the photograph stands a large, battered cooking pot filled with a purplish liquid. Behind the pot are broken chemical vials and bottles. Inside the pot is a fatal concoction of Kool-Aid and potassium cyanide. And spread out over the rest of the cover photograph are dead bodies. The corpses of those who followed the Rev. Jim Jones to Jonestown, Guyana.

Time correspondent Donald Neff, who flew over Jonestown, described the scene of this epic human tragedy with this report:

> The large central building was ringed by bright colors. It looked like a parking lot filled with cars. When the plane dipped lower, the cars turned out to be bodies. Scores and scores of bodies—hundreds of bodies—wearing red dresses, blue T shirts, green blouses, pink slacks, children's polka-dotted jumpers. Couples with their arms around each other, chil-

dren holding parents. Nothing moved. Washing hung on the clotheslines. The fields were freshly plowed. Banana trees and grapevines were flourishing. But nothing moved.

A human tragedy of such heartbreaking proportions! Nine-hundred-thirteen members of the People's Temple, dead in a self-imposed ritual of mass suicide and murder. And all of it at the behest of a fanatical demagogue. They drank the poison.

But it could never happen to you or me, could it? Which of us in our right mind would ever surrender our freedom of choice to someone who would eventually demand the ultimate sacrifice? We would never drink the fatal potion! We're simply too intelligent, discerning, and independent to let anyone do that to us. Aren't we?

And yet I wonder. Do we, too, drink the poison?

The three-letter poison

What about the three-letter poison called s-i-n? The ancient Scriptures declare that this solitary poison has always resulted—without exception or deviation—in what the coroner would declare a catastrophic terminal event, i.e., death. More potent than potassium cyanide and more pervasive, it is the single poison that has laid low the entire human race. Apparently there has been no one intelligent enough to forego or at least foreswear the drinking of this poison. Which includes you and me, doesn't it?

"Now, hold it right there," you may be protesting. "What're you talking about? I thought we just concluded in the last chapter that it doesn't pay to become preoccupied with sin, with this incessant worrying that we might have done something to offend God? After all, Dwight, your very premise is *outrageous grace*—that God cares for relationships more than rules. If that's the case, why get into a dialogue about sin and rule-breaking at all?"

That's a fair question. And I suppose I should apologize for even bringing sin up at all, since nobody talks much about it these days. While I write these words, my own nation is embroiled in a news media debate about the morality or the lack thereof regarding the president's personal behavior. And polls are clear that the majority of the American public would just as soon dismiss it all as unnecessary incursions into the private lives of public figures.

Maybe the question well-known psychiatrist Karl Menninger posed years ago in his best-selling book is still appropriate, *Whatever Became of Sin?* The one word, the single poison, nobody talks about anymore—"good, old-fashioned sin." Though of course there is nothing good about it, and it certainly hasn't gone out of fashion!

But does that mean that there is no such thing as sin anymore? Hardly! The fact is that while sin is a very popular thing to *experience* it's not a very popular concept to *explain*, much less talk about anymore.

But is it safe to quietly set sin aside on a dusty shelf somewhere and hope that by ignoring it, it will go away? I hardly think so, especially if we keep sneaking back to that shelf and sipping just a little bit of it now and then—for old time's sake. But the fact for everybody's sake is that sin is a poison as deadly as cyanide. That being the case then, doesn't it make all the sense in the world to boldly confront this fatal potion to ascertain its deadly truth?

What is it?

So what is sin, in your opinion? Feel free to check off the items in the following list that you would consider to be a sin:

- Is it a sin to drink a little wine now and then?
- Is it a sin to embezzle your employer's funds?
- Is it a sin to eat a chocolate chip cookie? How about to eat eight of them? What about twenty-three? What if you ate fifty-eight cookies in one sitting—would that be a sin?

- Is it a sin to be a workaholic?
- Is it a sin to engage in premarital sex?
- Is it a sin to engage in extramarital sex?
- Is it a sin to yell at your children?
- Is it a sin to cheat in school?
- Is it a sin to murder your neighbor?
- Is it a sin to murder your neighbor's cat?

How many times have you asked "Is it a sin to . . . ?"

But could it be that the reason we can't all agree on what is sin and what isn't sin is that we have a wrong concept of sin all together?

Let's return to the story we looked at in the last chapter, and consider the three characters and their understanding of sin.

The elder brother

He certainly didn't know it at all—didn't understand what sin is, and what it isn't. See him standing there in the middle of the barnyard in the midst of the lengthening twilight shadows. He stands there, his T-shirt drenched with smelly sweat, clods of damp earth clumped to the soles of his boots, smeared on his faded blue jeans, smudged on his glistening face.

He stands there; his back is aching. All day long he has bent over the steering wheel of that tractor, his callused hands sore from jamming that stubborn gearshift forward and back, forward and back.

He hurts! But he doesn't feel his pain right now. Know why? Because he's *had it!* He's had it up to here! All these years of backbreaking labor, and what does he get? Just look at what he gets! Over there, beneath the green, swaying poplars, is home sweet home. The windows are open. The orange light tumbles out onto the shadowed barnyard ground. The stereo is on—playing Dad's favorite Mantovani albums!

He can hardly believe his eyes—he doesn't want to believe what he is seeing. Mom and Dad and a few family

friends are in there, and they're throwing a party. Can
you believe it? Starting without him.

And what's the occasion? That good-for-nothing, no-
account brother of his has come traipsing back home, that's
all. He's been gone for months. Dad nearly bankrupted
the farm so that his boy could be free. And he went off
and had his good time, grabbed for all the gusto he could.
And probably slept with every woman in the city in the
process! Oh, but now the poor boy's tired of living without
his mother's home cooking. So he comes stumbling back
home. And what does Dad do? Does he give the boy what
he's got coming? Does he inform him that he's already
had everything the family owes him? Oh no. Not Father.
Dad goes wild instead in his excitement—calls up all the
neighbors, tells them to come over and welcome the lost
boy home! There'll be dancing and singing and food—the
barbecue's already stoked and started in the back yard.

Meanwhile what about me? the older brother fumes.
*I'm coming home too. But not from wasting myself in the
city. I'm coming home from another long, hard day of te-
dious work in the fields, and has anyone every thrown a
feast in my honor? Never! And they never will. Faithfulness, hard work, staying the course—it's plain these things
don't count in this family. Does Dad even come out to greet
me when I come in from the fields?*

Just then he hears the screen door slam shut, and he
peers through the gathering gloom to see who has come
out.

Sure enough, it's his father—hurrying down the walk
toward him now!

The big, burly older brother folds his bulging, bronzed
arms across his chest. His muddy boots stay planted, wide.
He looks at his father with steely eyes. The pressure cooker
that has been building up steam inside him every day he
has done two sons' work in the fields is about to blow its
lid.

The father is close now, arms outstretched. "Son, son,

I'm so glad you are back from the field. Have you heard the good news? Your brother has come home. He's here now—he's going to stay! Come in, quickly, get cleaned up, and join the celebration!"

We noticed the older brother's sullen, angry response in the last chapter: "I've been slaving all these years for you. I've never broken the rules. But what has it gotten me? Not even a measly little goat to slaughter for a sleepover. Nothing! But then this profligate, good-for-nothing low-life brother of mine comes staggering home, and what do you do? You empty the pantry, kill the calf we've been fattening for a festival, and invite the whole neighborhood in to celebrate! It's not fair, and I want no part in it!"

What is the elder brother's understanding of sin? We read it in Luke 15:29: " 'Listen! For all these years I have been working like a slave for you, and I have never disobeyed your command.' "

He's absolutely convinced that this is what the father wants—unquestioning obedience and the absence of wrong behavior. To him, sin is wrong behavior, and if he can convince his father that he has never done anything wrong, then nothing can keep him from procuring his piece of the pie.

The elder brother's concept of sin is behavior-oriented from beginning to end. He has a simple formula for success: The absence of wrong behavior guarantees success. Simply put—don't do anything wrong, and you'll get your reward.

But now the party music he hears streaming through the open windows of his home has thrown a wild card into the equation. Because here comes his kid brother who has literally done *everything* wrong, and he's still getting the reward!

The younger brother

But did the younger brother have any better, more accurate formula for life? Did he understand any better what sin is? Let's go back a day or two in the story and observe him and listen in on his thoughts.

There he is, standing there, a soggy cornhusk in each clenched fist. His legs spread eagle. His ankles sucked down into the oozing rot that lies like a sewage carpet on the pig sty floor. His nostrils burning with the wrenching stench that chokes his throat with a retching gag.

He's crying. The poor boy's cheeks are wet. And what does he mumble through his runny nose and salty tears? We can read Jesus' story in Luke 15:13-21:

"A few days later the younger son gathered all he had and traveled to a distant country, and there he squandered his property in dissolute living. When he had spent everything, a severe famine took place throughout that country, and he began to be in need. So he went and hired himself out to one of the citizens of that country, who sent him to his fields to feed the pigs. He would gladly have filled himself with the pods that the pigs were eating; and no one gave him anything. But when he came to himself he said, 'How many of my father's hired hands have bread enough and to spare, but here I am dying of hunger! I will get up and go to my father, and I will say to him, "Father, I have sinned against heaven and before you; I am no longer worthy to be called your son; treat me like one of your hired hands." ' So he set off and went to his father. But while he was still far off, his father saw him and was filled with compassion; he ran and put his arms around him and kissed him. Then the son said to him, 'Father, I have sinned against heaven and before you; I am no longer worthy to be called your son.' "

Do you see what the younger son's understanding of sin is? It, too, is very behavior-oriented. Ask the older son about sin, and he would start talking about *the absence of wrong behavior*. Ask the younger son about sin, and he speaks of *the absence of right behavior*.

Both sons are consumed with the behavioral model of sin. Both of them believe that the way to maintain or restore a saving relationship with their father is based on their behavior. The elder son feels he needs to demonstrate his absence of wrong behavior; the younger son hopes to win his father over by decrying the absence of right behavior.

But the father quickly demonstrates to them that they are wrong. And so are we, if we focus on behavior for our understanding of sin.

Remember our sample list of sin questions earlier in this chapter? Asking questions about sin like that demonstrates that we are just as behavior-oriented as the two sons were. Think about that list again: Is it a sin to . . . drink wine; embezzle; eat fifty chocolate chip cookies; engage in immoral sex? And on and on our sin-list questions can go.

Why? Is it because we want to be sinless? Do we create sin *lists* in an effort to be sin*less?* Do we really think that if we can come up with a comprehensive enough sin list, and avoid all the items on the list, that the effort will make us sinless?

That's the problem with the behavioral model for understanding sin. If we believe that sin is to be understood as engaging in forbidden behaviors, then surely the remedy for sin is behavioral as well. Surely the way to guarantee that heaven will throw a party in our honor is to avoid all the wrong behaviors we can possibly think of.

But let me warn you. That's the elder-brother trap. That's the righteousness-by-behavior trap. And Christians are forever getting caught up in that trap. Because we think sin is a behavior, we respond by basing the road to salvation on behavior as well.

Sin experts

It is precisely because of this notion about sin as a behavior that some communities, some marriages, some families, some churches, some schools have developed resident sin experts. Do you know any? I'm not talking about people who are experts at engaging in every imaginable behavior that we consider sinful. There are plenty enough of those in the world! But I'm talking about a different type of sin expert. People who have made it their life work to search out and point out sin. Resident experts on sin— on *your* sins, never *their* sins.

These are the souls who take it upon themselves to become the conscience for the rest of us. They scour the Bible and other Christian writings, compiling lists of sins, cataloging them for easy reference. They are usually the elder-brother type. And what they don't realize is that their negative, condemnatory attitude often has a lot to do with why the younger-brother types run away from the church, run away from God.

Of course, these elder-brother types never run away from the church, or from God—at least not visibly. It may be that they wish they could. It may be that they would give their eyeteeth if they could be out there partying with the prodigals. But oh, no, they would never do that. Because they're convinced that the only way to get a piece of the inheritance is to stay with the father and prove the absence of wrong behavior. No matter how you hate his rules, you've got to hang in there and endure him. ("Doesn't the Bible say something about 'he who endures to the end'?") Because in the end, elder brothers are convinced, right behavior (or at least the absence of wrong behavior) will bring you the reward you've been slaving for.

The problem, as we noted in the last chapter, is that such an attitude leads to such a joyless, sullen obedience. And that plainly spells a miserable existence. A miserable existence for elder brothers. And for everybody they live with—because misery loves company, and elder brothers work hard to enlarge their company! (If I can't be enjoying that, neither should you!) So out come the sin-inspecting magnifying glasses wherever they go.

Too bad their magnifying glasses aren't looking glasses instead! Jesus described people like this in Matthew 7:3 when He asked, "'Why do you see the speck in your neighbor's eye, but do not notice the log in your own eye?' "

What is it that drives people to be like this? What is it that drives husbands to pick on their wives and wives to pick on their husbands and parents to pick on their children and roommates to pick on each other and church members to pick on one another? Why are so many Christians so hard on each other? Pick, pick, pick, pick, pick!

Could it be that just like the two sons in the parable, we're stuck on the behavioral model of sin? If so, then we are just as wrong about sin and just as wrong about our Father as the two brothers were about theirs!

Sin and the father

Because have you noticed what preoccupies the father in the story? He is not nearly as concerned with right and wrong behavior as he is with broken relationships. The boys' model for sin is *behavioral*—the father's is clearly *relational*. If you were to ask the boys about sin, they would talk about broken behavior. But were you to ask the father about sin, broken relationships would be his concern. The father defines sin relationally more than behaviorally.

But I can hear someone protesting, "Wait a minute, Dwight. If you're inferring that the father of the parable is just like God, then what are you going to do with the classic Bible definition of sin, 'Sin is the transgression of the law' (1 John 3:4, KJV)?" Again, a fair question. And in response, reflect with me for a moment on the nature of God's law, the Ten Commandments. At their eternal heart, aren't all ten commands a divine protection of every relationship in this life that matters to a human being? The first four concern our relationship with God our Creator, and the last six revolve around our relationships with one another. At its heart the Decalogue is a relational document.

So if sin is the "transgression" or the breaking of one of those relationship-protecting commandments, then by definition and extension, sin is ultimately relational. Sin is first and foremost anything which threatens and breaks one of those protected relationships. Sin is any thought or behavior that jeopardizes either my vertical relationship with God or my horizontal relationship with another human being. Sin, in the beginning and in the end, is about relationships.

That's why when the father hurries out of the house to each of his sons, relationship and not behavior is what's on his mind. Because the pain of separation has been caused by a broken relationship more than some broken behavior. True, both boys begin their conversations by addressing their behavior. But notice that the father's response to both is to waive off their behavioral focus and with wide-open arms extend a relational offer. What Dad wants more than anything else in the world is to restore a deeply personal friendship with both boys. Period.

That's the way fathers are, you know. And that's the way our heavenly Father is too.

I know, because I'm a dad. Not a perfect father, to be sure, but I know how I love my kids and how I respond when my children fall or get hurt. I remember a time, a few years back now, when my children were small. I was taking Kirk, our energetic second-grader, to school one morning. We had a small two-door car, and so Kirk was in the back seat, since his little sister, Kristin, was strapped in her car seat beside me up front. (That was before the airbag days and all the accompanying warnings about putting our toddlers in their child seats in the back seat.) We pulled up to the school, I got out of my driver's seat so I could slide the seat forward so that Kirk could jump out.

Jump out, he did. Only he was in an eager hurry to

get to school, and so in springing out the door he didn't see my seat belt, which was hanging lose across the floorboard. And in that leap he caught his foot in the strap and flew through the air, tumbling headlong onto the concrete, his lunch box breaking open and spilling all over the pavement, his apple one way, his thermos another, and his sandwich yet another.

For a split second he lay there and I stood there frozen. And then he opened his mouth and sucking in all the air of the universe he let out a heart-rending wail.

Now, what do you suppose was going through my mind at that moment? Do you suppose I was thinking about Kirk's behavior? About how he should have been more careful? About how foolish he was to trip and fall? Are you kidding! The only thing this father had on his mind in that next instant was that my son was hurt and embarrassed and had need of only one thing: he needed me at his side, to reach down and scoop him up and hold him close and tell him that it would be all right. To embrace him and comfort him until the hurting and crying stopped.

And that's what this father did. And that's what our heavenly Father wants to do as well. Not just when we fall down and hurt ourselves physically. He wants to do it for us when we fall and fail spiritually and morally and emotionally.

Because when a child falls down, a father isn't thinking about the falling down, but the picking up and holding close. A father knows that what changes a child is not a lecture about behavior. What changes a child is the love of a relationship.

It is that way with our Father above. Look at him in this story. Why do you suppose he goes flying down the dusty road and slips the family ring back onto the finger of the prodigal son? Because a broken relationship needs to be restored! And why does he hurry out of the lamp-lighted house into the evening shadows to be with his elder son? Because a broken relationship needs to be restored. With both sons the driving motivation of the father is relational. For both his heart asks, How can I heal this broken relationship?

Relationships and redemption

And so it is with God. Jesus' punchline to the parable is inescapable. More than a tale about a younger or an older brother, it is the story about the Father. A Father who looks down upon a planet of children, His children, some who ran away from home and got lost, some who stayed at home and got lost, but all whose deepest need and truest thirst is for the Father. Augustine was right, "Our hearts are restless till they find rest in Thee."

So that we might find that healing rest, the Father bent low at Calvary to scoop us up and hold us close and offer to us in that crimson embrace of outrageous grace and relentless love all the healing and all the rest our hearts have ever wanted. "Come to me . . . and I will give you rest" (Matthew 11:28) those outstretched arms upon the middle cross till beckon. "Come home to Me, come home to My forever friendship, come home to My forever friendship."

The mysterious sign

I was deeply moved by a picture I saw in the newspaper some years ago. A picture of a mysterious sign that has appeared nailed to a tree near Nappanee, Indiana. It isn't one of those Madison Avenue billboards with smiling faces and catchy logos. Just a simple sign, with a few hand-painted words on it. And nobody knows from whence it came. Not even the farmer who owns the land and the tree upon which the sign is nailed. Three times the farmer has taken the sign down, and three times it has reappeared. You can't miss it, every time you round that curve in the road near Nappanee. It makes you wonder. Who put it up? Was it some heartbroken mother? A lonely father at midnight?

No one knows who put it up. But no one who reads it can forget it. Four simple words: "Son, please come back."

The same four words that God painted in crimson on a long ago tree. And a nailed-open embrace. "Child, please come back."

Isn't it time we stepped into that embrace and walked with the Father back into His house?

Chapter 4

How Do You Love a Consuming Fire?

It was a bizarre tale that unfolded in a town near Detroit, Michigan, just after New Year's Day in 1989. Leonard Tyburski was the dean of students at a local high school. He and his family lived in nearby Plymouth. But then one day in the fall of 1985, Mrs. Tyburski came up missing. A few days later, Leonard reported to local police that she had left, taking nothing but the clothes on her back. The couple had been married for seventeen years, but Leonard said that his wife had walked out after an argument, telling him she was going to go to Toledo, Ohio.

The police, of course, were immediately suspicious of Mr. Tyburski, since he was the last person who had seen his wife before her disappearance. They asked him to take a lie detector test, and he complied and passed. With no further clues to go on, the officers had to assume that Mrs. Tyburski was just another of the thousands of people who leave their homes every year in the United States and disappear into the woodwork, as it were. After all, it's a free country, and people have the right to go where they want when they want. After two years of investigation, the case was finally closed, and Mrs. Tyburski was listed as a missing person.

It might have stayed that way, except that the Tyburskis' daughter Kelly started having mysterious dreams about her mother. The rest of the story reads like something right out of an Edgar Allen Poe tale. Kelly had a recurring nightmare that her mother was in a place where she couldn't move—perhaps she was tied up or locked up. Try as she might, Kelly couldn't shake the feeling that the dreams were some sort of portent about reality.

There was the old family freezer down in the basement. They had used it to store meat up until the time of her mother's death. But then the key disappeared. Kelly became suspicious. She went to her father, but at first he couldn't remember where the key had been placed. But then he kept making up different stories about how the key got lost. And all the while Kelly's nightmare kept returning.

Finally, on Monday, January 2, 1989, more than three years after her mother's disappearance, Kelly decided to investigate for herself. Home alone, she got a crowbar and pried open the freezer.

She couldn't have been prepared for what she found inside. There, bent over the meat wrapped in butcher paper was her mother's frozen body. Leonard Tyburski was arrested on a new warrant and soon confessed to his wife's murder.

What a bizarre, shocking, utterly sad story. To think of that man living for three years with his horrible secret locked up in the basement freezer. Surely he must have had a hundred chances to dispose of his wife's body inconspicuously. But the haunting memory of his hidden sin must have been too much to face. So he left it and her buried in that cold, dark freezer in the depths of the place he and his daughters called home.

Bizarre. And yet it seems that even stories such as this have lost their power to shock us anymore.

Personal freezers

What has robbed us of the ability to be shocked or out-raged at such horrors? Is it the incessant fare of television, the movies? The constant parade of violence in our newspapers and on our newscasts? Or could it be that we each have our own freezer chests deep in the cold, dark basements of our hearts? Our own private collections of haunted fears and unsettling forebodings, our locked up guilts and anxieties. And as if that weren't enough, we must also deal with God.

To how many hearts is the memory of God an awful truth buried in that subterranean freezer? Because we have those moments, don't we? Solitary moments in some lonely motel room when we fumble in the bedside stand for that Gideon Bible. All we seek is a word of hope or reassurance or peace. Anything to stave the uneasy guilt or the anxious fear. But we are hardly ten pages into the Book before we run headlong into the God of the Old Testament. And suddenly a basement freezer chest of numinous fear rattles its locks and troubles our sleep. For three pages beyond the story of Creation begins a horrific litany of evil, of angry wrath and consuming fires, of raging floods and thundering voices, of burning bushes and searing winds, of bloody massacres and destroying angels. We meet once again the God of the Old Testament. And with a nightmare like that, who can sleep?

The God of the Old Testament. Who is this fearsome Being of those ancient stories? How can you possibly love such a God? How can you love a consuming fire?

And how can you possibly reconcile this vision with what we have described of the loving Father waiting with outstretched arms for His children to come home?

As we seek the answers, I invite you to journey with me to two long ago and far away mountains. Twin peaks we'll be scaling for the next few chapters. Two mountains

---

* I am indebted to theologian Alden Thompson for the two-mountains metaphor.

where humans have met the divine. Two mountains, one God. And one quest to know the truth about Him.*

A tale of three mountains

Our story actually begins on a third mountain, called by the ancients "The Mount of God."

Somewhere out there—beyond the black holes and white stars, there is a land and a kingdom high atop a shimmering mountain. It is the citadel of God, where once upon a long ago time there stood beside the Creator King a noble creature whose handsome beauty and princely bearing distinguished him as the head of all created life. His Creator Father named him Son of the Morning, Lucifer. And to this beloved child of His He gave the highest rank in the angelic orders—next only to God Himself.

But alas, it was there in the perfect heart of Lucifer that the mystery of evil germinated, springing to life from a dark and tiny seedling into a strangulating weed that choked his brilliant mind and throttled his innocent heart with the fatal insanity of self-worshipping pride. The mystery of evil's rebellion—who can understand it? I cannot. All that is left for us today is the ancient and tragic tale of that shattering angel rebellion that toppled the shining Son of the Morning into the hissing devil of darkness— Satan, that Old Serpent (see Revelation 12:7-9).

How shall we explain the mystery of rebellion? Can we blame it on God?

One afternoon, I made a pastoral call at the home of an elderly couple in my parish, two dear senior citizens who were great-grandparents several times over. Like the homes of so many proud grandmas and grandpas, they displayed a wall lovingly covered with the pictures of their seven children and even more grandkids and great-grandchildren. In a stroll down their memory lane, I listened as they told the stories about each of their seven children, stopping beside each of the high school portraits, recounting their lives and reporting on their present activities. Wonderful stories of service and faithfulness.

But then they came to the last child in the circle. The youngest. And a note of sadness crept into the voice of the mother as she told me the story. He grew up in the same home as the rest of the kids, the same family values, the same high standards. But for reasons nobody knew he turned his back on it all. Rejected them. Rebelled.

Imagine that family gathered together at Thanksgiving dinner family reunion. Six of the children have come home to be with Mother and Father. Laughter and smiles and joy all crowd around the family table. Father stands to pray a prayer of gratitude and thanksgiving. But what is it that trickles from the corner of Mother's praying eyes? A tear? But dear Mother, six of your seven children have come home—isn't that reason enough to be happy? But then we all know the universal truth—how can a Mother's heart ever be happy and whole when one of her children is missing?

And so it was about another family long ago and far away. One of the Father's children rebelled against everything the Family stood for and lived for. What went wrong? What was different? Same Parent, same home. But such tragically opposite results. God with Lucifer, these elderly parents with their lost boy—only love can know the depths of such a pain.

The mystery of rebellion

And it began in heaven. Where this most-glorious of the children began tiptoeing about the Home, putting his angelic arm around the shoulders of his friends and family, whispering the dark suggestion that God simply isn't all that He has made Himself out to be. Insinuating the doubt into minds willing to listen: God isn't a God of love— He just has us all fooled—we've been deceived by Him!

"Now if I were God." Rebellion inevitably moves to that pining wish, doesn't it? Pride acknowledges no second place. And the enchanted whisperings of the rebel angel were the promise of a higher existence than any angel heart had ever dreamed of—far away from the Father's laws and rules, far away from the "unquestionable higher authority" of such authoritarian rule. "Follow me," he hissed, "and we shall be as God!" And so they did, some of them. And the rest is history, the sad history that has entangled itself with the Earth story too.

Because what was a God to do? A heavenly Father?

Yes, it was fully within His power to instantly nuke His opposition and destroy Satan. But if You quickly destroy Your rebel child, You lose. Because the rest of Your children will now be convinced that Lucifer had been right all along—cross this "unquestionable higher authority" and He'll kill you, He isn't the loving God He's claimed to be. Oh sure, they'll worship You, but it will be the worship of hearts riddled with a new enemy called fear. And fear and love cannot coexist. In fact, the Bible declares that "perfect love casts out fear" (1 John 4:18).

Freedom to rebel

Which left the God of love with only one option. And here on the summit of this first mountain, the cosmic citadel, come the first glimpses into the nature of the Old Testament God, the forever God who was there before the Old Testament began.

God's only option: He chooses *not* to destroy His rebel child, Lucifer. Instead, God decides to grant to His adversary the precious gift of extended freedom, so that Lucifer might be given enough time to play out all the nefarious cards in his rebellious hand. And in that gift of extended time would come the revelation to the rest of the gaping, onlooking universe of the self-destructive insanity of a kingdom erected upon the pride of self-worship. Let the universe see that a rejection of the divine law is a rejection of divine love, which is but a rejection of divine life. Which is death.

And so the story went on to a once-upon-a-time brand

new planet in a swirling milky galaxy, chosen to become the theater of a cosmic life and death struggle between the forces of good and evil, love and hate, between self-sacrifice and self-preservation. Between God and Satan.

The rest is history. Sad, sad history. As a pastor, all too often I have to step into the pulpit and look down on a lone casket and a grieving family. I feel it every time—the pain of the history into which you and I were born. The story of life that turns to death in Genesis 3, with the heart-rending tale of Adam and Eve and a lost garden. And Cain and Abel. It was never supposed to have ended this way. But Lucifer won. Round One.

And the human race is sucked into the misguided notion in self-worship that self-actualization is promised. The forged lie of the forked tongue in Eden. And the story and lie go on and on and on. Belief that self-worship is where self-actualization comes from. It's a story that goes on and on. Like a broken record, the story of pain and death. Like a broken dam, the floodgates of human misery burst open and sweep their foul, brackish waters across this dying planet.

I don't know about you, but I hope that somebody out there in the universe is listening and watching right now. And taking notes on this tragic experiment in rebellion. I know that a few years ago the National Aeronautics and Space Administration launched Voyager II, an unmanned spacecraft now hurtling into outer reaches of space at ten miles per second. And should this craft encounter intelligent life out there, NASA scientists placed a gold-coated disk on board with the recordings of earth sounds (if the disk is played at 16 2/3 r.p.m.)! Just in case.

The watching universe

But I for one predict the intelligent life of this universe doesn't need a golden disk to ascertain the baleful results of rebellion. All they need to do is look at earth! This is the house that Lucifer built (or usurped). Let them stare long and hard at this cosmic theater, if they would know the woeful consequences of pride's hostage kingdom.

What is the handiwork of Lucifer they see, this rebel who promised them heaven if they followed? No golden disk here. Just a terrestrial collection of refugee camps with the bloated bellies and extended rib cages of starving children. War, with its carnage that strews the maimed and the dead in its global wake. Evil with its unspeakable holocausts that mute an entire civilization. Human beings, created in the image of God, who stuff each other's bodies into locked up basement freezer chests. The promise was heaven. The delivery was hell.

All because Lucifer longed to be God.

And where was God, where is He in all this nonstop heartache?

Standing heartbroken by the gates of an empty garden. Standing all alone, His children all gone. The same Father who stood on the verandah of the prodigal's home, day after day, anxiously squinting toward the horizon, hoping against hope that his boy might come home. The same Father who hurried into the dusky shadows of the barnyard to urge his other son to come in, to step back into the circle of his family love. Same Father. Still standing, still waiting.

Six chapters into the Genesis story, He's still standing, still waiting, by the way. "The LORD saw that the wickedness of humankind was great in the earth, and that every inclination of the thoughts of their hearts was only evil continually" (Genesis 6:5). Because generations after Adam and Eve the story has gone from bad to worse! Once again the divine Parent comes in search of His children, and what a sorry, sorry encounter! ". . . only evil continually." What's a God to do? A Father?

He doesn't lose His temper and throw a megaton tantrum. How does He respond? Read the next verse: "And the LORD was sorry that he had made humankind on the earth, and it grieved him to his heart" (verse 6).

Is this a picture of an angry God? No, it is a picture of a sad, sad God. A brokenhearted God. Crushed with pain, filled with grief. And do you know why? Because only love can be heartbroken. Only a heart that knows love knows pain. No love, no pain. And God's heart is filled with love; it is filled with pain.

The lie about God

But somehow, despite all of this love and pain in the heart of the divine Father at the very beginning of the Old Testament, we have gotten the wrong picture. Instead we have gotten a picture that the devil himself has painted for us, the very one who has continued to slither through time, insidiously whispering in our ears, insisting that God has ruled human history with a coldhearted, heavy-handed leash, dragging us against our will, scaring us out of our senses, destroying us at his capricious whim. It has been a divine reign of terror, the devil taunts. After all, look what He did in the Flood!

All right, then. Let's do it. Let's take Satan's challenge. Let's examine for a moment how God has handled human history. Let's take this Exhibit A that the devil keeps throwing up in God's face. What about the Flood?

In my Bible the story of the Flood comes immediately after the words we just read from Genesis 6:6. Words that tell of a God whose heart was filled with grief and pain.

Picture Him with me for a moment. Picture Him standing all alone at the gates of Eden—the very garden He had joyously created to be the paradise home of the new human race for eternity. A garden that now lies as silent as the grave, empty of its human inhabitants since the banishment of Adam and Eve and the lying serpent. God stands alone at the gates. And as the generations go by, He looks out over the earth and realizes that every inclination of the thoughts of human hearts is only evil all the time. You can't get any worse than "only evil all the time"!

So what can He do? What are His options? If He lets

this cancer of sin continue to grow unchecked, the very life of the planet is at stake. He must take invasive action. He will lose it all unless the cancer is excised.

I still remember the phone call I made a few years ago to a friend of mine, a building contractor who had built our previous home for us, on the other side of the country. In our conversation he told me about the disturbing pain he had developed in his leg a few months earlier, a pain that wouldn't go away. After a battery of tests at Stanford University, the diagnosis came back: cancer of the bone. The doctors treating him had two options: let the cancer remain and metastasize throughout his entire body, or take immediate, radical, invasive action to destroy or cut out the cancer.

What do you suppose was their choice, his choice? In order to save his life, there could be only one choice—eradicate the cancer before it spread

The truth about God

Would it be any different with God? I remind you that the God we meet in the story of the Flood is the very same God who first created Adam and Eve for companionship, for a forever friendship. The same God who later walked with Enoch, as Enoch walked with Him. The same God who has always hungered for the love of His children, who longs for their salvation, who thirsts for their companionship. It is no wonder that we find this heartbroken God aching and hurting as He watches His children who would rather be slow-dancing with the devil than life-walking with their Creator. If they were your children who had run away, wouldn't your heart be breaking too?

But not all of them had abandoned Him. There were still a few faithful children who hungered for His companionship and love.

But if the cancer of rebellion is allowed to continue to grow out of control, God will end up losing them, too, thus losing the entire human race. So, you make the call. You be the doctor. Are you willing to cut off the hopelessly diseased portion of the body in the urgent effort to save the life? Or do you spare the diseased portion and lose everything?

You choose.

Nobody said it would be an easy choice.

But when the whole organism is being ravaged toward a painful death, what else can you do?

Let's read the account once again, of how God responded:

"The LORD saw that the wickedness of humankind was great in the earth, and that every inclination of the thoughts of their hearts was only evil continually. And the LORD was sorry that he had made humankind on the earth, and it grieved him to his heart. So the LORD said, 'I will blot out from the earth the human beings I have created—people together with animals and creeping things and birds of the air, for I am sorry that I have made them.' But Noah found favor in the sight of the LORD." (Genesis 6:5-8)

And so the God who stands all alone by the gates of His empty garden searches the land for a loyal friend through whom He might still save the human race, or at least a small part of it. Someone who might go to the lost world and plead the invitation of God: Come back to Me, come home to Me, come to Me that you might be saved. In a white-bearded, ark-builder named Noah God found His friend and sent His appeal.

The very same appeal we hear over and over again through the Old Testament prophets whose appeal is sounded from one end of the testament to the other: If you want to live and be saved, come to Me. Come now. I can't wait forever. If I do, I'll lose the whole race. " 'Turn to me and be saved, all the ends of the earth! For I am God, and there is no other' " (Isaiah 45:22).

These are not the words of a consuming God. They are the plea of a compassionate Saviour.

A pile of wooden planks in the form of an ark was the offer of His love back then. A pair of wooden boards in the form of a cross is the expression of His love today. Nothing has changed.

It's the same God.

It's the same love.

It's the same urgent plea.

It's the same final decision—to cut out the cancer before the race is lost.

It's the same clock counting down to eternity.

It's the same arms outstretched in love.

It's the same merciful invitation.

"For as the days of Noah were, so will be the coming of the Son of Man" (Matthew 24:37). No wonder the invitation hasn't changed: Come home. Come back to the Father before it is too late.

That's the truth about God. And the Flood. And the divine heart that was forced to choose to eradicate the disease before it destroyed the entire human race. Radical, invasive action. To save the life. It cost a death. Eventually His own death.

Come home. Come back to the Father before it is too late.

Nothing's changed. Which means the final choice and the last decision is up to you, up to me. Knowing what it has cost God from the beginning to make the invitation, what good reason could there possibly be to *not* respond to His offer just like Noah did?

"Noah walked with God" (Genesis 6:10).

Chapter 5

When the Gun
Is Aimed at You, Jump!

I was a young pastor, overflowing with enthusiasm for introducing people to God. I was teaching a Bible class for new Christians, journeying through the great themes of the Bible, exploring what the Bible says about God and how we should live in relation to Him. We were having a great time. And then one day one of the class members brought his sister to class with him.

I'm always delighted to have visitors, so I welcomed her warmly. But then as I launched into my topic for the day, she raised her hand. And I knew I was in for trouble!

It was one of those uneasy questions about the God of the Old Testament—very much like the questions I mentioned in the last chapter—questions about the very nature and character of God in the light of some of the Old Testament tales. And so, she asked, what kind of a God is this you teach people about?

My mind scrambled. Then I smiled. Not to worry. After all, I was a young minister just a few years out of the seminary, and I had been trained with all the right answers. And so I gave her one. And I could tell she didn't like it. But the class must go on, and I did.

After class I approached her and, with the gallantry of a young preacher, I offered to visit her the next week and pursue her question further, confident to myself that she'd see the light with a little more Bible study. She agreed.

And so it was I showed up at her doorstep, armed with the Word of God and prepared to set this errant heart on the straight and narrow regarding the truth about God.

One slight difficulty, however: She was ready for me! I had hardly been seated, when it became rapidly apparent to me that this young seeker wasn't quite ready to play the role of meek and mild learner at the feet of this great teacher! She was loaded for bear! She had done her homework. In the Bible. And she unloaded both barrels blazing straight into my theological defenses!

"What kind of God is it that you're teaching to people—vengeful, angry, fiery, bloody, judgmental, cruel. . ." She took a breath. And I hurriedly threw in one of my prepared answers. No good. She fired on. "What kind of God is He who rules His followers through force and fear?" She took another breath. I tossed out another prepared response. Still no good. And I quickly ascertained that every time she breathed she was simply reloading her cannon. And this young preacher was quickly becoming cannon fodder. Which left me with the final solution—the "fodder" away I could get the better!

So, beating a hasty retreat I mumbled something about another appointment and went home. Theological tail between my legs.

Years have gone by now since that ignominious day, but the questions didn't go away as easily. Serious questions I needed to find answers for, answers that would satisfy me, answers beyond simply what others had taught me.

At the time I didn't think I would ever thank God for that embarrassing encounter, but looking back now, I am grateful for the questions that I faced that day. Her withering broadside forced me to dig deeper.

Looking for better answers

Because over the years I've faced similar questions over and over again. What kind of a God does the Bible call us to worship, to serve, to love? A gentle Jesus meek and mild, or a fiery Father wrathful and wild?

In the intervening years the questions haven't changed. What's changed are my answers. Because through the years my own understanding of God has changed. Which hasn't necessarily left me with *all* the answers. But the answers I have found are settling some of the questions I, too, have asked.

Which is why I've invited you to join me in this journey into the heart and soul of God. Let's face the questions together fairly and squarely. Let's not run from them this time.

In fact let's turn to the most terrifying theophany in all of Scripture. Do you know what a theophany is? It comes from a Greek word made up of two parts *theos*, which means God, and *phainein*, to show. It refers to a showing, or an appearance of God to a man or a woman. For the next several chapters we're going to focus on the theophanies of God on two very different mountains.

We already gazed up at "the mount of God" in the last chapter, and that of course was a third mountain, located somewhere out beyond the Van Allen belts of outer space. But now let's climb a mountain right here on planet Earth. Mount Sinai. The jagged, rocky summit where God came down to deliver His Ten Commandments to the human race. Without question it is the place of the most terrifying theophany recorded!

The mountain of terror

Just three months before this fated Mt. Sinai theophany, in a predawn moment of sheer madness, the children of Israel had fled for their lives. For generations they had been the brutalized slaves of the land of Egypt. But now under the cover of darkness in the mighty Exodus they become a horde of liberated slaves. And they leave behind them a land in utter devastation.

It had all begun with the sudden appearance of a shepherd named Moses, himself a fugitive from Egypt for forty years. But he has returned. And in a glow of a still-fresh encounter with the God of Abraham, Isaac, and Jacob, Moses came striding back to his enslaved people with the electric announcement that the God they had forgotten all these decades had not forgotten them. And He was about to set them free!

Pharaoh was adamant. Never! But in a blistering succession of ten crippling plagues, each one launched against another vaunted god or goddess in Egypt's pantheon, the God of Israel brought that proud and mighty monarch and nation to his knees in the stunning conviction that his national gods were impotent impostors. There is only one living God!

And with that shout, Israel escapes the clutches of Egypt. Straight through the Red Sea on dry land, mind you, with Pharaoh's pursuing army drowning right behind them! All the way to the dusty feet of Mt. Sinai, it was a heady string of supernatural interventions and miraculous deliverances. Manna out of the sky and water out of the rocks. What a God!

What an awesome God! What a fearsome God! You'd hardly want to cross Him, now would you?

And now word has buzzed through the camp that this omnipotent Being desires to meet with His children. To talk to them, to really *talk* to them! In a few days He will personally descend to the craggy peak of Mt. Sinai. "Prepare to meet your God!"

Come with me to that unprecedented, unforgettable moment of meeting—that theophany—recorded vividly in Exodus 19:10-13, 16-19:

> The LORD said to Moses, "Go to the people and consecrate them today and tomorrow. Have them wash their clothes and prepare for the third day,

because on the third day the LORD will come down upon Mount Sinai in the sight of all the people. You shall set limits for the people all around, saying, 'Be careful not to go up the mountain or to touch the edge of it. Any who touch the mountain shall be put to death. No hand shall touch them, but they shall be stoned or shot with arrows; whether animal or human being they shall not live.' When the trumpet sounds a long blast, they may go up on the mountain."

On the morning of the third day there was thunder and lightning, as well as a thick cloud on the mountain, and a blast of a trumpet so loud that all the people who were in the camp trembled. Moses brought the people out of the camp to meet God. They took their stand at the foot of the mountain. Now Mount Sinai was wrapped in smoke, because the LORD had descended upon it in fire; the smoke went up like the smoke of a kiln, while the whole mountain shook violently. As the blast of the trumpet grew louder and louder, Moses would speak and God would answer him in thunder.

Have mercy!

Ever awaken in the middle of a rainy spring midnight? It happens all the time here in Michigan. Startled out of your wits by a roaring clap of dark night thunder, you lie there, slowly awakening to the reality of the storm that is beating against your window panes. Suddenly the bedroom lights up like a blinking neon sign, white light through the closed curtains. And instinctively you begin the count, "One lollipop, two lollipop, three lollipop . . ." as you try to calculate the distance of that lightning bolt. Five seconds and then the crash of the thunder, no problem, it's a mile away. But what happens when your midnight bedroom blazes with white lightning and before you can mutter "lollipop" at all, the thunder clap explodes outside your window!

Now hold that exploding lightning in your eyes and ears and then throw in a 6-point Richter earthquake beneath your feet, and for good measure have some mysterious trumpeter blasting his horn in ear-splitting decibels— and you have the supernatural ingredients of the frightful theophany upon Mt. Sinai that fateful day! Anybody feel like running yet?

It's no wonder the children of Israel were sternly warned not to touch or even get near the mountain on pain of death! It was a holy place, a terrifying place. Made so by the rumbling, exploding presence of their God!

It's no wonder that even Moses quaked in his sandals. "Indeed so terrifying was the sight that Moses said, 'I tremble with fear' " (Hebrews 12:21).

"For indeed our God is a consuming fire" (Hebrews 12:29).

But why does He reveal Himself in this way?

In the previous chapters we have seen Him as a relentless lover—the Father, hungry for a relationship with His children. Doing whatever He can to bring them home to Himself.

But this vision we get here at Mount Sinai seems a galaxy removed from the "gentle Jesus, meek and mild" (as the old hymn sings) we have come to love. This is fire, raging, consuming fire.

Why did God choose to paint this kind of self-portrait to the thousands of children He had just delivered from slavery?

Meeting us where we are

The answer to that question, I believe, reveals one of the most stirring truths about our God. *He is the God who meets us where we are, and takes us as we are!*

Remember who it is He is dealing with here. A mob— a sprawling, throbbing mob of runaway slaves! A liberated nation of slaves just released from nearly two centuries of bloody slavery. A people whose every move, almost every thought, has been dictated by the whip. People who, for the sake of sanity and survival, have been forced to accommodate themselves to fear, compulsion, blind obedience. A people whose reflexes respond best to brute force.

Oh, sure, four centuries earlier their ancestor Abraham had walked with God, had even communed with Him face to face. But in the passage of time, after the death of Isaac and Jacob and Joseph, the flickering light of the knowledge of God was nearly snuffed out by the cruel lashes of Pharaoh's taskmasters. Their liturgical system was gone. The spontaneity of devotion and adoration to God was nearly extinguished by the pagan oppression of Egypt.

But God hasn't forgotten them. The time has come for Him to rekindle the dream, to reignite the hope, to restore a nation that will love, trust, and follow Him wherever He leads. But liberated slaves are the fodder for His dream. What is a God to do? A Father?

Ah, He is the God who meets us where we are and takes us as we are. The prodigal father with his two boys. The thundering God with His thousands of slave children.

And so, for a nation of liberated slaves just three months old, God rivets their undivided attention with the most spectacular and terrifying sound and light show this earth has ever witnessed. Because in a few moments He is going to write with His own finger, upon tables of stone, the eternal principles of His kingdom of love. The Ten Commandments.

Somebody had better be listening when He gives the Ten Commandments! So, He first gets their attention. Then He speaks to them in a language they understand. For generations they have been living with stern prohibitions—the lash of the whip whenever they step aside from the prescribed path. They thoroughly understand negative commands. Don't do this . . . don't do that . . . under the penalty of death!

And so, when God comes down to meet with His set-free children, He doesn't come and quietly whisper in their ears "Now, I want you to be honest today, be kind to each other, be pure, be loving, because I am love." They weren't ready for that. They haven't seen love and honesty and purity lived out as an example to follow for centuries!

So God says, "I'll speak your language then." He thunders from the fiery, smoking, trembling mountain: DO NOT STEAL! DO NOT LIE! DO NOT MURDER! DO NOT COMMIT ADULTERY! because it will kill you!

The people respond

And when God spoke their language, they got the message, because God got their attention! "When the people saw the thunder and lightning and heard the trumpet and saw the mountain in smoke, they trembled with fear. They stayed at a distance and said to Moses, 'Speak to us yourself and we will listen. But do not have God speak to us or we will die' " (Exodus 20:18, 19 NIV).

God had not only gotten the attention of this vagabond troop of wandering, liberated slaves. He had literally "put the fear of God in them!" They pleaded with Moses to go and speak with God as their representative, and to bring His words back to them. They were scared almost to death!

Now that God had their attention, He had Moses explain this frightening theophany to them. It wasn't to make them afraid of their God. It was simply a test—a demonstration designed to indelibly impress upon them the reality of God's grandeur, His glory, His holiness—a passionate self-revelation from their Liberator to turn them from their enslaving sins, to turn them back to the only One who could keep them free!

Which is precisely what Moses himself instructed the people in order to allay their fears and teach the truth. Listen to Moses' illuminating response to the people's trembling fear: "Moses said to the people, 'Do not be afraid. God has come to test you, so that the fear of God will be with you to keep you from sinning' " (Exodus 20:20 NIV).

"You don't have to be afraid of God," Moses encourages the children. "Be afraid of sin! It is sin that will kill you!"

Isn't there a better way?

But couldn't God have found a better way to communicate this message to His people? What about the second mountain? Why didn't God give the Israelites Mt. Calvary there in the barren wilderness, instead of Mt. Sinai? Why didn't He move straight to the most glorious summit of all time? After all, what more dramatic revelation could there possibly be, for slaves or freedmen alike, than to witness sin's bloody, brutal crushing out of the life of the world's Redeemer? Why didn't God give them the broken heart of Jesus atop Calvary's cross, rather than the exploding thunder of Sinai's summit?

I find my answer to that question at the salad bar.

Let me explain. One of the great inventions of restauranteurs has been the salad bar. Now on-the-road menus are no longer limited to a predominantly greasy-spoon kind of selection. Sprawling, well-stocked salad bars mean you can practically eat as nutritiously on the road as you can at home. Which is why our family has taken refuge in these wonderful inventions whenever we've traveled by car from coast to coast.

But when Kirk and Kristin were young, Karen and I quickly discovered that when it comes to salad bars and kids, along with the boon comes the bane. Because typically most salad bars come equipped with a super-duper dessert bar! Which being interpreted means that you can't turn your kids loose in a salad bar without close parental supervision! Why? Because given the choice, kids will go for the sundaes long before they turn to the salads!

And my two kids love ice cream.

Which is why when our children were quite young, and we'd come stretching and yawning out of our small car into a salad bar restaurant, you know where their eyes would instantly be riveted? You guessed it—on the beckoning all-you-can-eat self-serve ice cream dispenser, with its one hundred chocolate-and-cooky-and-candy toppings side counter.

Now suppose I had wanted to be a gracious, caring, loving father, and I didn't want to set down any arbitrary, harsh-sounding rules. I could have just taken my two children to the salad bar, and pointed out all the broccoli, carrots, cabbage, and coleslaw, and extolled to them the wonderful merits of the vitamins, minerals, and roughage in those foods.

But trust me on this. I could have commended the good till I was blue in the face, but it would have gone in one little boy, little girl ear and out the other. Because all my kids had on their little minds was the swirling ice cream machine down at the end.

So we gave our children all the freedom in the world . . . to begin at the broccoli bar. No broccoli, no ice cream. No cauliflower, no cake. Period.

How could parents be so ruthless and cruel? Ah, because a parent knows that his child doesn't have enough information yet to process an intelligent, life-preserving choice. I can't *commend* broccoli to that little mind, so I just *command* it instead!

Now, they've grown older, they have come to understand the merits of broccoli on their own (even though former President Bush still renounces it!). They've both matured to the point they can make an informed and wise choice whenever they step up to a salad bar. And we no longer have to command them to eat the good.

That's the way God worked with His children at Mt. Sinai. If He had come down to them as the gentle Jesus, they likely would have trampled Him into the dust of that valley, and gone on about their sinful lives with no consideration at all of the God who loved them. Spiritually, they were but babes, possessing insufficient knowledge on which to make intelligent, life-preserving choices.

Without something to shake them up and rivet their attention, they would have gone their own way, and would have spiritually starved to death.

And so God, the all-wise and all-loving parent, made their salad-bar choices for them as He started them on their road to spiritual health and spiritual maturity. Before they could encounter their Saviour, they must encounter their sins! Hence Moses' reassuring explanation in Exodus 20:20—You don't have to be afraid, just recognize that God has done this to keep you from sinning.

He is the God who meets us where we are and takes us as we are.

Who's to blame?

Do you realize, because of that commitment, the incredible lengths that God will go to in order to communicate with you and me, to win our hearts? Watch what else He does with the children of Israel!

Did you know that out of love for those ex-slaves, God carefully omitted any mention of the fallen angel who became the enemy of heaven and earth? In fact, in the first five books of Moses Satan is mentioned by name not once! Nowhere in the opening stories of Scripture does God mention Satan or blame him for any of the evils that the people suffered. In fact, Satan gets very little mention at all anywhere in the Old Testament.

Have you ever wondered why this is?

Remember, once again, from whence the people had come, these children to whom God was speaking at Sinai. They've escaped the land of Egypt—a land whose shadowy religion boasted a pantheon of deities, good and evil. Now that His children are set free, God must liberate them from any temptation to polytheism, the worship of many gods. And so rather than mention Satan and risk their worshipping him as the god of evil—as the surrounding nations did—God deliberately chose to assume full responsibility for all the mess sin has caused. So committed was

He to meeting them where they were and taking them as they were, He took the rap for evil Himself!

And so we read in Exodus that God hardened Pharaoh's heart, even though it was in fact the self-destroying pride of Lucifer that steeled Pharoah's heart against God. Throughout the five books of Moses, God Himself is the One who takes the blame for disease, destruction, and devastation. Not one word of the enemy we now know is the cause of all evil. God was patiently willing to wait until His children were more mature to understand a fuller explanation of sin and evil. For now He would let them blame Him for the actions of the fallen rebel angel.

And to think that all these years you and I have wagged our fingers at this "Old Testament God" who hardens Pharaoh's heart just so He can kill him. But we've been wrong, terribly wrong about God. Because all this time, quietly, without protest, God has borne the brunt of our blame. All because He loves His children that deeply.

God is so in love with us that He is willing to meet us where we are, and take us as we are!

I don't know how you describe it, but it occurs to this feeble little mind that the God I meet at Sinai, the God I find throughout the Old Testament, is a God whose heart passionately throbs with love for His children, all of them, you and me included.

Jump or I'll shoot!

Which puts a whole new angle on some very old stories!

Take the story Charles Spurgeon used to tell.

It's the long ago story of the captain of a large man-of-war sailing ship, who would occasionally take his young son with him on some of the sea-faring voyages. The boy had a pet monkey, and the two of them loved to scramble up and down the rigging of that large sailing vessel.

One stormy day the monkey scampered up the rigging with the boy fast behind. Higher and higher up the ropes they climbed, until finally, shinnying up the mast, they crawled up onto the little round platform, or main-truck, at the top of the mast.

Climbing up onto that platform was one thing. Getting back down quite another. The ship was pitching and rolling violently, and as the boy tried to climb back down, he found that his legs were too short to grasp the mast below him. Clinging to the mast for dear life, the boy was trapped. Weary from the race up the mast, his grip on the mast was weakening. He wouldn't be able to hang on much longer. Each pitching roll spelled his certain doom, for if he fell to the hard wooden deck below he would be dashed to death.

His father looked up and with horror saw his boy's predicament. There was only one hope. The boy must jump from the mast during one of the pitching sways of the ship in order to fall into the foaming ocean, where the sailors could rescue him. Otherwise he would plunge to his death on the deck below.

Quickly the captain called for the speaking trumpet and yelled up to his boy, "Son, the next time the ship rolls to the right, throw yourself into the sea!"

The poor boy was petrified. It was a long, long way down past the deck to the heaving waves below. And he just could not bring himself to let go and jump for his life. But neither could he hang on for much longer.

In desperation the captain called for a gun. Raising its sights, pointing it directly at his son, he called out "Boy, the next time the ship rolls, jump into the sea, or I'll shoot you!"

The boy knew his father meant it, and when the ship lurched again he leaped into the roaring waves below. Out shot the brawny arms of a sailor, hauling the dripping lad back to safety. He was rescued.

Throw yourself into the sea, or I'll shoot you! "When the people saw the thunder and lightning and heard the trumpet and saw the mountain in smoke, they trembled with fear" (Exodus 20:18 NIV).

There are times in our human pilgrimage when thunder and lightning, earthquake and fire, are the only language that can save us. Times when it takes something drastic to get us to leap to safety, to jump to life.

If that is where you find yourself today, don't give up! Because in the midst of the storm is a Father who is desperately wants your attention. "Throw yourself into the sea or I'll shoot you," is but a last-ditch, earnest, loving appeal to drop into His strong, loving embrace.

Atop Mount Sinai, He aimed His thunder and lightning at us and cried, "Jump for life!" But atop Mount Calvary the thunder and lightning were aimed at Him, and He cried, "I am your life!" The thunder and lightning fell on Him too.

Which is proof enough that if you climb either mountain today, it will be the same love that meets you at the summit. No wonder a friendship with this same God is a mountain-top experience!

Chapter 6

The Executioner

Tuesday, January 24, 1989, a pale looking forty-two-year-old law school dropout, wearing a light blue shirt and dark blue pants stepped into a small chamber that had only a single piece of furniture. Both his head and his right leg had been shaved.

Looking frightened, he walked directly across the chamber and sat down in the plain wooden chair. Assistants fastened the belts and buckles that strapped him in place and attached electrodes to the shaven spots on his head and leg. Checking the wires that led from the electrodes to a secluded panel, they then hurried from the room.

The man in the chair nodded to his attorney, and to his minister, who had spent the night with him in prayer. "I'd like you to give my love to my family and friends," were his last words. At 7:06, six minutes past schedule, an anonymous executioner released 2000 volts of electricity. Behind a Plexiglas partition, forty-two witnesses watched.

Ted Bundy, the confessed murderer of twenty-three young women, and a suspect in dozens more slayings, gently arched back in the electric chair and clenched his fists. One minute later the electricity was shut off. At 7:16

Bundy was pronounced dead.

And the world cheered.

Outside the Starke, Florida, prison a crowd of 300 had gathered, carrying placards with macabre slogans: "This Buzz For You!" "Roast in Peace!" "Thank God It's Fry Day!" Residents of Lake City, Florida, cheered. It was in their community that the body of twelve-year-old Kimberly Leach had been found in an abandoned pigsty in 1978, a victim of Bundy's pleasure-crazed insanity. They all cheered.

The disk jockey at a nearby radio station had been encouraging his listeners to shut off all their appliances at seven that morning, so the executioner would be sure to have all the "juice" he needed. The world seemed pleased to be rid of Ted Bundy.

All except one person. Three thousand miles away on the opposite coast was a woman who had received Ted Bundy's last telephone call. It was his mother. And into the telephone she breathed the assurance, "You'll always be my precious son."

Thank God it's fry day?

Is God the one we have to thank? And I'm not thinking of the execution of Ted Bundy now. I'm referring to the six or eight troubling execution tales recorded in the Bible. They appear to be supernatural executions. Moments when a man or woman is suddenly stricken by death, and rather than giving an organic or human cause for the death, the ancient record attributes it to an act of God.

What shall we do with those stories, if we are going to tell the truth about God? How do they possibly fit with the stories we've already been examining? Stories of the open-armed Father who keeps pleading with His children to come home. Who meets us where we are and takes us as we are, all with the passionate hope to win our hearts and friendship in the end.

But what about these tales of execution? Shall we like the proverbial used-car salesman resort to some fast-talking distractions in hopes the customer never sees the major ding on the far side of the car? Does God need used-car sales techniques to sell Him? Shall we hide the stories? Or do we dare to be honest and share *all* that the Bible has to say about Him? Bluntly speaking, if we're honest how can God come out smelling like a rose?

But then again, the Bible is not a garden of roses. It's much more than a pocket full of posies. Ashes, ashes, we all fall down! The question is Has God fallen too?

A New Testament execution

Let's consider one of these execution stories in particular. I've chosen this one because it's found in the New Testament, after the death, resurrection, and ascension of Jesus. This story is not found in the gray, sober shadows of the Old Testament. Found in Acts 5, this story comes in the glow of the early, triumphant, glory days of the new church that Jesus has founded.

Everything seems to be flowing along splendidly for the church. It's a time of miraculous power and spontaneous joy, despite some early opposition and persecution. The growth figures are phenomenal. People are working together in harmony and peace. There are no poor among the Christians, for those who have houses and lands are selling them and distributing the proceeds among the believers. Nobody's hungry. Everybody's happy! To throw in an execution story at this point would bring the party to a screeching halt!

And yet, like a funeral pall, Acts chapter five slashes across the spiritual ribbons and balloons with its tragic tale. Let's relive the moment and reflect on its meaning. The story begins simply enough in verse 1: "But a man named Ananias, with the consent of his wife Sapphira, sold a piece of property." Ananias' Hebrew name was Hananiah, which means "The Lord is gracious," or "The

Lord is good." His wife's name, Sapphira, is the Aramaic word meaning "beautiful." So, here is a story about a man named God is good, and his wife, beautiful. How ironic their names for so tragic a tale.

There's a key word in the verse that ties it back to what has gone before. The word is *but*, and it links us back to the end of chapter four, where a man named Barnabas had sold a field that he owned and had brought the money to the apostles. The very mention of Barnabas' generosity suggests that his gift was looked upon quite favorably within the fledgling Christian community. So, it appears that part of Ananias and Sapphira's motivation for what they did was to be able to bask in some of that same favor as well. After all, a little philanthropy now and then certainly doesn't hurt one's standing in the community!

But the plot thickens in verse 2: "With his wife's knowledge he kept back some of the proceeds, and brought only a part and laid it at the apostles' feet." Now, we must recognize that there was nothing wrong with selling the land and there was nothing wrong with keeping a portion of the proceeds. It was their land, after all. They could have kept the full amount and been totally within their rights. Bringing any of the proceeds to the apostles was a matter of freewill generosity.

But it seems that they wanted to have their cake and eat it too, as the saying goes. And so both of them together came up with the scheme to take only part of the money to the church, but to claim that they were giving their all for the cause of God. Then everybody would heap favor and accolades upon them for their generosity, while unbeknownst to the rest, Ananias and Sapphira could enjoy the hidden profits for themselves. You might call it a greedy little leveraged buyout, a little bit of insider trading, just a little something to pad their own pockets while their philanthropy is glowingly reported!

It's interesting to notice that the words translated "kept back" in verse 2 are the same words used in the Greek translation of the Old Testament story of Achan, the man who "kept back" certain of the spoils of Jericho for himself and brought disaster upon the newly formed nation of Israel. It's also a word that's used by the apostle Paul in Titus 2:10 to mean stealing.

Somehow, with uncanny discernment, the apostle Peter sees through the couple's perfidy. He looks into Ananias' eyes and reads his heart: " 'Ananias,' Peter asked, 'why has Satan filled your heart to lie to the Holy Spirit and to keep back part of the proceeds of the land? While it remained unsold, did it not remain your own? And after it was sold, were not the proceeds at your disposal? How is it that you have contrived this deed in your heart? You did not lie to us but to God!' " (Acts 5:3,4).

Notice here that Peter gives Ananias a chance to set the record straight. He asks four questions, and each time Ananias could have broken down and confessed the whole truth. But Ananias never takes the opportunity. He has decided on a course of action, and it's as if he's decided he's going to stick with it even if it kills him!

"Oh, Ananias, you aren't playing this game with us," Peter's point is inescapable. "You're playing a game with God, and it's no game at all, the act of lying to the Holy Spirit." In fact Jesus called it the "unpardonable sin." Which in the end is any sin the heart refuses to yield to the pleading voice of the divine Spirit through the human conscience.

The next words of the story are shocking: "Now when Ananias heard these words, he fell down and died. And great fear seized all who heard of it. The young men came and wrapped up his body, then carried him out and buried him" (Acts 5:5, 6). Our first reaction might be to attribute his death to a sudden cardiac arrest brought on by the shock of being found out, and that would be a plausible conclusion were it not for the even more shocking ending to the story.

"After an interval of about three hours his wife came

in, not knowing what had happened. Peter said to her, 'Tell me whether you and your husband sold the land for such and such a price.' And she said, 'Yes, that was the price' " (Acts 5:7, 8).

This is Sapphira's second chance to pull out of the devilish scheme. She could have protested her husband's deceit in the first place, but she chose to keep silent. Now Peter gives her a chance to confess their veiled deception, but like her husband she has decided to stick to their story.

Share the lie, share the proceeds. Now she shares his fate: "Then Peter said to her, 'How is it that you have agreed together to put the Spirit of the Lord to the test? Look, the feet of those who have buried your husband are at the door, and they will carry you out.' Immediately she fell down at his feet and died. When the young men came in they found her dead, so they carried her out and buried her beside her husband. And great fear seized the whole church and all who heard of these things" (Acts 5:9-11).

Executioner God?

So, what kind of a God is this, anyhow? A husband and wife decide to help out the church, but lie about the exact amount. And suddenly they're dead within three hours of each other. A strange coincidence? Hardly. The very fact that Acts records the story, along with reporting the fearful reaction of the church, indicates that the incident was widely viewed as an act of intentional divine judgment on Ananias and Sapphira

What kind of God is this? One we should be afraid of, or one we should be a friend of?

If that were the only incident of supernatural death recorded in the Bible, we probably could find some way to explain it away. But nobody has to remind us that there are nearly a dozen more such stories in the Old Testament. Among them the familiar stories of Nadab and Abihu, the two eldest sons of the high priest Aaron. They were slain by fire because of irreverence in the sanctuary.

Add to that the story of Korah, Dathan, and Abiram, and those that followed them in rebellion against Moses—literally buried alive when the ground opened up and swallowed them. Uzzah died for touching the ark. Nearly 200,000 Assyrian soldiers were slain in the night by an angel of the Lord. All of these stories depict these deaths as supernaturally caused as the result of divine judgment.

How on earth can we correlate these acts of human execution with what appears to be the competing portrait of God as the caring, pleading, waiting Father? Jesus himself announced, "'Whoever has seen me has seen the Father'" (John 14:9). Is the gentle Jesus the divine Executioner?

These questions have troubled me personally, and I have had to restudy and rethink the stories, in search of a possible root meaning to all these accounts of God's sudden and dramatic interventions to take life rather than give it.

I have finally found an answer that settles it for my heart, and I'd like to share it with you.

Unconditional love and freedom

The answer swirls in the turbulent caldron of unconditional love and unconditional freedom.

You may remember a song that was popular a few years back. One line went something like this: "I'm gonna make you love me, yes I will, yes I will!" But how foolish can you get! You can't make anybody love you. The idea is wrong, dead wrong, 180 degrees wrong. Because, sir, if you force that woman to love you, it won't be love at all. You know it; she knows it. And that's the truth for you, too, ma'am.

We all know the truth about true love. And that is, in order for love to be love, it must grant you the right to say No, as well as the right to say Yes. No freedom to say No, no love. Period.

Enter now the three words of 1 John 4:8—"God is love."

Agape love, in the Greek, which means unconditional, self-sacrificing love. Which also means that God knows what every desperate husband or wife knows who's trying to win that partner back from divorce.

As a pastor I hear the heartache stories over and over. And so I know the desperation of a jilted heart that wants to win back what was to have been its life partner. Oh, if only love could be forced, then there would be no divorce. But the painful truth is that there would be no love either. Not if it were forced.

And so God granted the human race the right and the freedom to say No to His love. And say No we have. In the Old Testament we said it, in the New Testament we said it, in today's testament we still say it. No, God! Or sometimes, no God.

Through the words of the prophet Hosea, you can almost feel the pain in God's heart as He cries out like a jilted lover in the face of another No: "When Israel was a child, I loved him, and out of Egypt I called my son. The more I called them, the more they went from me; they kept sacrificing to the Baals, and offering incense to idols. Yet it was I who taught Ephraim to walk, I took them up in my arms; but they did not know that I healed them. I led them with cords of human kindness, with bands of love. I was to them like those who lift infants to their cheeks. I bent down to them and fed them" (Hosea 11:1-4).

And how did the people respond to this loving care? "My people are bent on turning away from me. . . . How can I give you up, Ephraim? How can I hand you over, O Israel?" (verses 7, 8)   You can sense the deep emotional struggle going on in the heart of God. "How can I let you children go?" How He wishes He could win back the love of those who have written Him off and run away from the home of His love. Woo them, win them, but He cannot force them. Love won't. He must give them up.

And in most circumstances, in normal circumstances,

God does just that. He lets the rebellious, defiant heart go. And by the billions human hearts have turned away from Him through the course of history. How many have gone to their graves unchecked and unhindered by divine judgment, exercising their divinely given freedom to say No right up until the last dying moment. God let them go.

But there have been crisis moments when the very survival of God's handful of loyal people on earth has been at stake, as was the case in the Flood story we examined a couple of chapters back. In crisis situations like this, drastic action is imperative. It is God's only recourse.

Accelerated judgment

Enter now once again the tragic execution tales, and what I have come to call God's "accelerated judgments."

Accelerated judgment—what does that mean? It means that the God who reads our hearts can see each choice and the ends to which our choices naturally lead. Now that we live in a world practically ruled by the computer, such a notion is hardly novel! If computers can calculate the many variables in a particular circumstance and even predict the outcome on the basis of all those variables, isn't it possible for the omniscient God of the universe to do the same? Of course!

The fact is that seeing the direction our choices are leading, time and again God has interrupted our lives. Why He even used a talking donkey once upon a time to get a man's attention and arrest his course of action! And it worked! Just as dramatically as it would with you, were you reading your evening paper and suddenly your pet dog started chatting with you! Come on, there isn't a one of us who, once we'd recovered a semblance of coherence, wouldn't listen *very carefully* to what our dog had to say to us!

Throughout the checkered history of God's children on

earth, He has resorted to very extreme measures to arrest their attention and reverse their direction. But if they kept retorting No, No, No, No—what was a God to do? A Father? Listen to His heartbroken cry: "Ephraim is joined to idols—let him alone" (Hosea 4:17). For seven centuries He had tried to woo back Israel, Ephraim. But now there is nothing more He can do. Their No is final.

What a sad, sad day when the God of the universe has to utter those words: "It's all over." "There's nothing more I can do for him." "She's said No to Me forever." "There is *nothing more* that I can do." "Leave them alone."

But in the midst of ebb and flow of divine wooing and human responding, there were isolated critical times when God did not have the luxury of waiting. Crisis times when the survival of the very community of faith was at stake. Crucial times when it was imperative that God step in and speed inevitable consequences up. I call them times for God's *accelerated judgment*.

The execution stories already mentioned in this chapter—those drastic moments when God Himself stepped in and acted suddenly, causing death among His people—as I've gone back and reexamined these stories, I've discovered two very important characteristics.

First of all, every one of those people—Nadab, Abihu, Korah, Dathan, Abiram, Uzzah, Ananias, Sapphira—had been a witness of supernatural divine intervention—at the Exodus, at Sinai, in Canaan, at Pentecost. Each of these knew well the story of God's loving guidance; each had learned of His protective laws of love. But in spite of what they had seen and what they knew, they still had turned their back on God and said No.

Moreover, in every one of those cases God extended more than one opportunity for them to turn to Him. But in the face of it all, they said No to God. A review of all their lives is sufficient evidence to conclude that divine love had sought every option to reach their recalcitrant hearts. The answer to Him was clearly No.

Understanding the heart of God

But there is an even more crucial second characteristic in these execution tales. And that is that in every case the life of a fledgling community of faith was at stake. If those Nos were allowed to spread, the entire community would have been jeopardized and potentially lost. God *had* to intervene drastically and quickly!

Remember the old proverb, One rotten apple spoils the whole barrel? Well, it's true, biologically and spiritually. When I mentioned that proverb once in the pulpit of my university congregation, one of the biology professors, Dr. David Steen, wrote me a letter the next week detailing the scientific hows and whys of that old proverb. I won't burden you with the four paragraphs detailing the chemical reactions in apples (called the "climacteric"), but apparently even "a mere whiff of ethylene (a common air pollutant put out by both automobiles and industry, not to mention other plants [it is also a plant hormone]) will cause a mature but green apple to go into the climacteric." And when one apple goes into the climacteric, new ethylene can quickly penetrate the other apples, sending them into rapid maturation (a euphimism for spoiling)! As Professor Steen wrote, "Indeed one rotten (ripening) apple does spoil the whole barrel. When you find the rotten apple it is usually too late though. The rest have already been gassed."

And what is true biologically is true spiritually.

Which is why the heart of divine love was so quick to act when the spoilage of one of His children threatened the rotting of the entire community! Because rebellion is contagious.

But isn't God a God of freedom? Don't we have the right to rebel?

Yes, indeed we do. But do we have the right to destroy the right of others not to rebel? When does my saying No need to be terminated so that others get the right to say Yes? If the festering rebellion is allowed to spread, the whole organism will be contaminated.

When cancer begins to invade and multiply in a human body, we are faced with a similar choice. Do we spare the life of a cancerous lung at the expense of the entire body? Or do we radically remove the diseased portion in order to save the whole? In essence, doesn't every life-saving surgeon choose to take the life of the lung in order to save the life of the patient? Spare the lung, lose the life. Paint this decision in the context of love and ask the question: Which is the most loving response—to spare the lung or to spare the life?

In the case of Ananias and the others, divine love had no choice. It made the wrenching decision to take the life of the few. In order to spare the life of the many.

And so God exercised accelerated judgment. He already knew, He could already see where their personal choices were headed. But in these few instances He could not afford to let their rebellions take their natural courses and wait until the final judgment. Too much was at stake. The lives of too many of His children were at risk. And so God simply but drastically stepped in and accelerated those choices to their inevitable end. He gave the rebels what they had chosen—separation from Him—He gave them their ultimate freedom—but separation from the One who is life is always death. Accelerated judgment.

It was the wrenching decision of relentless love.

Do you think it was an easy decision? Do you think it was easy for God to take those lives?

Consider another story. Watch another Man, all alone, stumbling up the side of a mountain. When He reaches the summit, He lies down and stretches out His arms. And dies. Nailed between heaven and earth on a bloody cross.

Why does He die?

He dies so that a rebel planet will forever remember the wrenching decision of relentless love. To save the life of the many it cost the life of the One. Accelerated judgment. In your place, in my place.

Thank God it's Fry Day they said of Ted Bundy's death.

Thank God *for* Friday I say about Jesus' death.

Chapter 7

The Ayatollah and God

Perhaps you remember the story of Salman Rushdie, the author of a book called *The Satanic Verses*. Up until 1989 he was a rather obscure author, a British citizen of Indian descent living in England. In the fall of 1988 his book was published, and it received fairly positive critical acclaim. But it didn't make a big splash in the book world. Most people had never heard of it. I doubt that many Christians rushed out to purchase it, given its title.

The book probably would have sold only a few thousand copies and then would have gone the way of most books quietly out of print, except for one moment of totally unexpected notoriety. In February, 1989, the 88-year-old leader of Iran's Islamic fundamentalists, the Ayatollah Khomeini, stepped up to a microphone in Tehran and spoke these ominous words: "The author of *The Satanic Verses* book, which is against Islam, the Prophet, and the Koran, and all those involved in its publication who were aware of its content, are sentenced to death."

And—as you can well imagine—Salman Rushdie's book became an overnight, runaway international best seller, flying off the shelves of bookstores around the globe. No one could keep it in stock. And Rushdie probably would have been laughing all the way to the bank were it not for the fact that with the Ayatollah's death sentence came a $5.2 million bounty! And if that weren't enough, the Ayatollah also issued his personal promise that any Moslem who killed Rushdie would be guaranteed entrance straight into paradise itself!

Rushdie, of course, went straight into hiding, for the world learned long ago that the threat of Islamic death squads is no laughing matter! He also immediately did the prudent thing—issuing a public apology for the turmoil and distress his book had caused the Islamic world.

The world waited to hear whether the Ayatollah would call off his secret executioners.

Just a day later, the Ayatollah issued this statement: "Even if Salman Rushdie repents and becomes the most pious man of all time, it is incumbent on every Moslem to employ everything he's got, his life and wealth, to send him to hell!"

And lest you think that the now deceased Ayatollah's railing condemnation of Rushdie has abated and been forgotten, the new Speaker of the Iranian Parliament, Ali Akbar Nateq-Nouri, in a speech to the parliament on the ninth anniversary of the late Ayatollah's pronouncement against Rushdie, renewed the death sentence of the British author as a lesson—in his words—to "those who oppose God and God's prophets."

What kind of God?

It makes you wonder, doesn't it, what kind of a god such a religious leader must envision and embrace. What kind of a god refuses to forgive? What kind of a god condemns a man straight to hell with no opportunity to make amends and start over again?

Is the God of the Bible a god like that? Unrelenting in His punishment of sin? Unforgiving in His pronouncement of death? The Voice in the microphone of human conscience that announces there will be no reprieve, to hell you go?

We've examined together some of the troubling stories of the ancient Scriptures. Execution tales, supernatural catastrophe stories. And I hope you've concluded with me that these were rare cases of accelerated judgment—hardly typical of God's patient and merciful ways.

But there are other troubling stories in the Bible as well. Ones that don't fit that pattern all that well. Take the one found in a book of long-ago history, Numbers chapter 20.

Remember Moses? He is well remembered in all three great world religions—Judaism, Islam, and Christianity. But when we come upon him in this incident, Moses is an old man, certainly by our standards, nearly 120 years old to be exact. By now he's given forty years of back-breaking, heart-rending service to God and His children of Israel. He has wandered all around the mulberry bush, so to speak, with a stiff-necked, belly-aching mob of whiners. For forty years! He could have been in the Promised Land thirty-eight years ago, had it not been for the people's faithless rejection of his and God's leadership. But Moses had pleaded with God to spare those rebellious ex-slaves. And God had answered His friend's passionate intercessions, with the sentence that children of Israel must wander forty years in that barren wilderness until the last of the faithless rebels had died off. Only then would Israel be ready to follow God into Canaan.

For nearly four decades now, Moses has had to trudge through the hot desert sands, waiting and waiting and waiting. And while the rebel parents and grandparents have died off, Moses has inherited their kids. And guess what—they're no better than their parents!

Thirst in the desert

I must confess to you that when I come to this sad, sad

story in Numbers 20, I have a hard time, a very hard time, accepting the way the story ends. I mean, what kind of a God is it that we find here? Moses has given forty years to You, God, and then You end the story like this? After all he's done.

Review this difficult story with me in search of what we might learn about God. Is He like the Ayatollah, harsh and unforgiving? What would He have us believe about Him from a story like this?

The story opens with a crisis: "Now there was no water for the congregation; so they gathered together against Moses and against Aaron" (Numbers 20:2).

Remember, something very similar has already happened nearly forty years earlier. And on that day God had instructed Moses to strike a rock, and fresh cool life-sustaining water had burst from the rock to slake the thirst of the people and their livestock. That was forty years ago. And it's not like they've been wandering around ever since with their parched tongues hanging, dying of thirst all these years. Hardly! Fact is, God has been miraculously providing for their needs every step of their wandering way. Not only water, but food as well. And they are now practically on the borders of the Promised Land. Just a little longer to go!

But how quickly we all forget the providential provisions of God! And so God tests the mettle of this new generation's faith. He lets it appear that their water has dried up. Will they recall His grace and goodness over the decades? Or will they melt down into bitter, faithless, rebellious complaining?

God didn't have to wait very long for the answer!

Sadly true to hereditary form, just like their parents, they turn on God, and hurry to the tents of Moses and Aaron, wagging their fingers, pointing, poking at those aged beards, blaming God and His servants for their unhappy predicament. "The people quarreled with Moses and said, 'Would that we had died when our kindred died before the LORD! Why have you brought the assembly of the LORD into this wilderness for us and our livestock to die here? Why have you brought us up out of Egypt, to bring us to this wretched place? It is no place for grain, or figs, or vines, or pomegranates; and there is no water to drink'" (Numbers 20:3-5). Talking about "*deja vu* all over again!"

Poor Moses and Aaron! After forty years of thankless leadership, is this what it has come to? They've given their hearts, and now they get it in the neck! Criticized, scandalized, harassed, and blamed. The last time the people complained about water, they were ready to stone the two of them.

You know, Oswald Chambers was right. In his wonderful little book *My Utmost for His Highest* he describes the high price of ingratitude that leaders must face: "If we are devoted to the cause of humanity, we shall soon be crushed and broken-hearted, for we shall often meet with more ingratitude from men than we would from a dog."

How true it is! And so, poor Moses and Aaron, these two aging brothers, the leaders of God's people, come stumbling out of their tents. Where can they go? Who can they turn to? They are the leaders—there's only One to whom they can turn. Running across the hot, dry sand, racing to their place of refuge: the tent of the assembly—the sanctuary-church where they often met with God. Exhausted, frustrated and hurt, they cast themselves on their faces before God. What do we do now? "Then Moses and Aaron went away from the assembly to the entrance of the tent of meeting; they fell on their faces, and the glory of the LORD appeared to them" (Numbers 20:6).

The glory of the Lord appeared to them! Isn't that a touching scene? Here they are, prostrate, utterly defeated it would seem, and then a bit of the glory of the Lord like a shaft of light shines down upon them with the glowing reminder that God is still God and He is still in control. A whispering reassurance, as it were, straight from His heart to their worn, weary souls—"It's OK, friends. I'm still on My throne. And you can still count on Me."

What a God! Just when you think you're at your rope's unraveled end, He comes down—way down—close to your confused, battered heart. And you hear His voice—"It's OK, friend. I'm still God. I'm still on My throne and still in control of your life. You can count on Me. Trust Me!"

And with that assurance, God has very specific instructions for Moses and Aaron: "The LORD spoke to Moses, saying: Take the staff, and assemble the congregation, you and your brother Aaron, and command the rock before their eyes to yield its water. Thus you shall bring water out of the rock for them; thus you shall provide drink for the congregation and their livestock" (Numbers 20:7, 8).

God speaks from a heart of love and concern and instructs Moses to do the same—go to a rock and speak to it in the name of the Lord.

And here is where I keep wishing I could rewrite the rest of the story! Even if it meant rushing up to Moses' side and clamping a hand over his mouth before he utters a word. But alas, every time I read of this moment Moses opens his mouth before anybody can stop him. Not even God.

And Moses loses it! "So Moses took the staff from before the LORD, as he had commanded him. Moses and Aaron gathered the assembly together before the rock, and he said to them, 'Listen, you rebels, shall we bring water for you out of this rock?' " (verses 9, 10). And the damage had been done!

Moses' eyes blaze out over that angry sea of faces. Most of these grown up kids were knee high to a grasshopper forty years ago when the pilgrimage had begun. Now look at them. In disbelief Moses stares into their agitated faces. You'd think that after four decades of non-stop miracles and divine intervention they'd have learned the lesson that you can count on God no matter what's happening in your life right now!

But have they learned that lesson?

Certainly not!

And so, meek and gentle Moses, nearly 120 years old, has finally had it up to here! The elderly gentleman explodes! Raising his staff up the brassy heavens, he raises his voice, louder and louder. Four decades of pent-up frustration erupt like a volcano. "Listen to me, you rebels! What do you want *us* to do? Haven't we taken good care of you these last forty years? Huh? Have you ever starved? Have you died of thirst? NO! You have not! Why not? Because we've been here for you. Given you everything you've needed. Well, I'm just sick of this. I've had it with the whole blooming mess of you!

"You want water? Well, I'll get you water. Stand back, you rebels!"

And with that, poor, tired, old, angry Moses whirls around on his worn sandal, and raising the sacred rod of God high overhead, Moses slams it down with a furious WHAP! against the wilderness boulder. He spins around to glare at the crowd. Then still enraged with the pent-up anger of four decades with this whining mob of ingrates, poor Moses crashes his rod across the face of the rock again.

And in that instant an explosion of water bursts forth from that rock, like an artesian well.

The people screamed with delight and rushed to the water, dancing and singing and splashing. Not far behind, their flocks and herds lunge for the refreshing cool. With laughter and bellows human and beast wallow in the gushing new stream.

But Moses stands to the side. Alone, he leans on his staff. He watches. He trembles. You know how it is to be angry—so furiously angry that the adrenaline rushing through your system sets your whole body to shaking.

I don't know how long Moses stood there watching, thinking, wondering what would ever become of this foolish, faithless people. But finally he left that scene, heading back toward his tent, and on the way he passed by the tent of assembly. And as he stepped past it, he must have heard the voice of God speaking to him, perhaps in only a whisper time: "But the LORD said to Moses and Aaron, 'Because you did not trust in me, to show my holiness before the eyes of the Israelites, therefore you shall not bring this assembly into the land that I have given them'" (Numbers 20:12). Because of your actions, I am *not* going to let you cross over into the Promised Land. Period.

What a heartbreaking ending to a story that began with two men throwing themselves on the mercy of God and performing such a wonderful miracle of preservation for God's people!

The story ends with the somber but cryptic words of verse 13: "These are the waters of Meribah, where the Israelites quarreled with the LORD and where he showed himself holy among them" (NIV).

The holiness of God

The place where the Lord showed Himself holy! What in the world does that mean? If that is how the Lord shows Himself holy, how is He any different from the Ayatollah Khomeini? It hardly seems fair, does it? Moses and Aaron with forty years of a nearly spotless record, now make one mistake, and God says That's it! One strike and you're out! No trip to the land of promise for you!

How is that so different from the Ayatollah's death decree for Salman Rushdie—no matter if he repents, he still deserves to be sent to hell!

Considering all the evidence you and I have already examined, is there no way to harmonize this snapshot of God with all the other portraits of His we've contemplated here? Or is this sad story a tragic tale that's been preserved to teach us—Look out, because God can throw the book at you over a single sin?

But think with me for a moment. Is this really a story about Moses and Aaron and God's harsh reaction to a single sin? But how could it be? If this were a story about the two of them getting nailed over a single sin, then it's a bit late, wouldn't you say?

Look at Aaron. He already has at least two biggies on his record already! Remember when Moses was up on Mount Sinai getting the Ten Commandments from God. Where was Aaron? Down in the valley molding an idol— a golden calf—for the forgetful slaves. And when Moses returned and asked Aaron what he had done, all the high priest of God could come up with was the lame mumbo jumbo about throwing the crowd's jewelry into the fire, and *poof!* out came this golden calf!

That *was* a big sin, a very big sin—and one that he wasn't willing to admit and confess even when God gave him a chance. Instead he concocted a story to cover his failure, much like Ananias and Sapphira did centuries later.

But that wasn't his only sin. Because later Aaron collaborated with his sister Miriam in rebelling against the God-appointed leadership of Moses. Miriam contracted leprosy, Aaron a very severe reprimand. Over the years God has been extremely gracious, loving, and patient with this elderly gentleman.

And so God has been with Moses too. If this story is to teach us that God kicks people out over just one sin, then it comes forty years too late in Aaron's life, and it comes at least *eighty* years too late in Moses' life. Because it's been that long since Moses murdered an Egyptian taskmaster. And a litany of other failures would include all of Moses' faithlessness and excuse making in response to God's call, his failure to circumcise his sons. No, this sin at Meribah is not the first in this man's life, either.

The fact is, God has been very patient and loving with both of these two elder statesmen of Israel.

Responsibilities of leaders

Could it be we've had this story all wrong? Could it be that at its heart the issue in this tale is *not* the character of Moses and Aaron?

Oh yes, there *is* an important lesson here about the responsibilities of leadership, to be sure. Because no matter what face you put on this story it is a very somber word of caution and warning to leaders, isn't it? There is a towering price and sobering cost for all spiritual leadership.

There have been enough fallen television preachers in the news over recent years to remind us all of the destructive hemorrhaging that can result from one leader's single sin!

When Moses in rage lost control of himself in front of all the people, he gave them the "perfect" excuse for their own fallen lack of self-control. After all, if this great man of God loses it, how can anyone expect anything better of me? I mean, come on, if the leader sins, what's the big deal if I sin too? He's the one who gets paid to walk and work with God full-time. If he can't help himself, how can I?

Isn't that the way our misery-loves-company human nature keeps consoling itself? The tragic word filters through the ranks of God's people that one of His leaders has fallen, and what do we all do? We breathe a sigh of relief and secretly congratulate ourselves that our sins certainly aren't that bad, or at least aren't any worse than his, than hers.

I repeat—there's a tragic hemorrhage of righteousness, a tragic loss of good, whenever a leader falls, for a leader seldom falls alone. Others fall with him or her.

When Moses fell, the entire forty years of his leadership and God's providence were immediately called into question and challenged. Everything he has written, said, done, became suspect in the eyes of the people. With one rash act of passion, it was all threatened. Such is the fallout from a leader's failure. The people at last had an excuse to rationalize their own rebellious sins.

Yes, there is an important message for leaders here.

But could it be there is an even greater truth embedded in this story? More than a tale about the characters of Moses and Aaron, could it be a compelling portrait about God? A portrait that in the end bears no resemblance at all with the Ayatollah?

The truth about God

Perhaps the cryptic clue to the truth we seek is found in what appears at first to be a contradiction. Doesn't verse 13 seem to be entirely out of place? It reads, "This is the place where the Lord showed Himself holy to the people." But wait a minute. What did God just say in verse 12? He announced to Moses and Aaron, "You did not honor Me as holy in this place." Verse 12 says they didn't do it, but verse 13 says this is the place where God was shown to be holy.

How can we possibly reconcile these two verses?

As I wrestled with this story again, I realized that the apparent contradiction hinges on that word *holy*. The holiness of God, what is it? Isn't it the character of God?

And what is the character of God?

We've heard it many times: 1 John 4:8, "God is love." But how can you find love here?

Take a look again. Because God's holy love comes shining through. God actually reveals His love in its ultimate purity in this story!

And here is how: God lets the rebels cross over, but He keeps the leaders outside. So that the people would never forget, as long as they lived, the high cost of His outrageous grace and His relentless love, He lets them cross over but refuses the two leaders entrance.

It's hard to believe, isn't it? But then, isn't that just like God? Isn't that exactly what He did at Calvary? What happened at the cross? Once again: He let the rebels cross over, but He kept the Leader outside—outside the gate on a bloody Roman cross.

Outrageous grace, relentless love.

You see, God never treats us other than He is willing to be treated Himself. So Aaron will die on one mountain top, and Moses will die on a second mountain top, and God will die on a third mountain top. So outrageous His grace, so relentless His love.

And so the story ends with the words "And Moses buried Aaron at the top of the mountain."

A few weeks later it is Moses' turn to die, but now there are no leaders left to bury him. Nobody except of course the One who has been Moses' leader, Moses' Lord, and Moses' love for all those years. It's as if God says "Never mind that there is no one left to bury Moses. I will bury My friend Myself."

And so God did.

I've often wondered what that moment must have been like. Perhaps you've seen the Harry Anderson painting depicting that scene. There is Moses, bushy eyebrows, gray beard, leaning upon that worn staff at the summit of Mount Nebo, staring into the gathering gloom about that mountain top, his longing eyes peering off into the purpled distance toward the Promised Land. This is all he will see of it. So take a good look, Moses.

And then with a deep and wistful sigh Moses slowly lowers himself to the ground and leans his tired back against the rock. The Rock! All through the dusty years of his desert wanderings the Rock has been the symbol of His Lord, His God. And now he leans all his weight upon His Saviour. He has repented of his sin a hundred times, I imagine. And he has been assured of his forgiveness just as many times, I'm also sure.

And so now the tired warrior leans against the Rock and falls asleep. Asleep in the arms of One who will never let him go.

The Bible declares that God buried Moses, but remember, it also reads God raised him! The Lord didn't let Moses sleep in death for long. Because before long, he feels a hand shaking his shoulder arousing him from the slum-

THE AYATOLLAH AND GOD   101

ber of death, "Moses, wake up! Wake up, My sleeping friend. It's been lonely without you around here. And so if it's all right with you, I've come to take you home. Home to the real Promised Land. Home to My forever friend-ship. Welcome home, My fallen friend. My forgiven friend, come on home!"

Outrageous grace! Relentless love!

Because when you have a piece of the Rock, you have the promise of the Redeemer. Forever.

Chapter 8

Why God Can't
Sleep at Night

M. Scott Peck's book *The Road Less Traveled* has stayed on the bestseller list for longer than any other book in history. Psychiatrist Peck's opening salvo is three words long: "Life is difficult."

But then you don't have to be a rocket scientist or a psychiatrist to recognize the truth of those three terse words, do you?

I live in a small rural community, half of which consists of the university campus that I serve as pastor. Whenever I hear sirens in the distance, I catch myself instinctively tensing and wondering if they wail for someone I know. Chances are they often do.

One such morning I was hurrying my children to school, when up ahead I saw the flashing lights—red lights, blue lights, there obviously had been some sort of accident on the main road through our town. Dropping my kids off at the school, I raced back to the intersection and pulled off the road near the pick-up truck and passenger car collision. I spotted the chief of police standing in the midst of the shattered glass and crumpled metal. Knowing him, I hurried over to inquire the identity of the victims. The chief pulled out the driver's license of the woman victim— "Do you know her?" Of course I did—she was the wife of one of our university faculty. "Then would you please get a hold of her husband and inform him his wife has been seriously injured?" How serious, I asked. "It doesn't look very good."

I raced down the side lanes to campus, grabbed a telephone, dialed his office, and when he answered, tried to keep a steady voice, "Bill, your wife has been in a bad car accident. They're transporting her to the hospital right now. Meet me out front of your building. I'll take you to her."

In anguished silence Bill sat beside me as we raced to the emergency room. There was little I could say or tell him. Silent prayer was all that was left for the two of us. Finally into the silence he blurted out, "Oh Dwight, I hope to God it doesn't happen again." Again? "We lost our young son, when he was struck while riding his bicycle . . . I can't lose her too."

The ambulance was empty in front of the ER doors. We raced inside. Behind the curtain doctors were frantically administering CPR. Bill, himself a medical professional, pushed through the curtains. But the resuscitation efforts were futile. Her life was gone. His wife was dead.

In numbed silence I later stood in some hospital anteroom with him. It had happened again.

"Life is difficult."

Every siren that wails, every telephone that rings is the potential harbinger of confirmation that Peck is right, "Life is difficult."

And death is the ultimate of life's crushing difficulties. As a pastor it is in the presence of this universal enemy of the human race that I must stand, casket after casket after casket. Three caskets for three young twenty-something men, young professionals, off on a ski weekend to

Wisconsin in a private plane that froze over on take off and crashed causing three tragic untimely deaths. Three funerals back to back. Three broken and devastated families.

"Life is difficult."

One casket for a four-and-a-half year old little angel who valiantly battled her leukemia unto the very end. Tears were all that was left.

Life can be very difficult.

One casket for a beloved grandmother who on a happy December morning was off on a Christmas shopping spree for her loved ones, until the head-on collision just three miles from her front door. With another police officer, I stood at that front door minutes later, the messenger of shattering tidings for her disbelieving husband.

One casket for a three-week-old baby boy, whose heart was supposed to last at least three score and ten years like most of the rest of us. But didn't. A broken, grieving family left behind.

Small caskets, long caskets, young caskets, aged caskets, it doesn't matter. "Life is difficult."

Where is God?

So, where is God in all of this? In the twisted face of human suffering, where is the God who is the shining hero and blessed assurance of Psalm 121: "I will lift up my eyes to the hills—from where will my help come? My help comes from the LORD, who made heaven and earth. He will not let your foot be moved; he who keeps you will not slumber. . . . The LORD will keep you from all evil; he will keep your life" (vv. 1-3, 7).

Keep my life, your life? From all evil? He will? Then what went wrong with all the stories we just shared? They were all good-hearted, even God-hearted men and women and boys and girls. And yet they suffered. In the words, once again, of best-selling author Harold Kushner, "when bad things happen to good people." How they have suffered. But why?

Is it because God was slumbering? After all, the psalmist declares that because He doesn't slumber we don't suffer. So is it axiomatic then that when we do suffer it's because He has slumbered? That hardly seems rational in the light of the character of God we've been examining in these pages.

So why evil? Why is life so very difficult? How can you possibly defend a good God in the midst of such awful evil?

That is the question implied in the word *theodicy*. It's a scholars' word to describe the human heart's attempts to, somehow, in the presence of evil and suffering, defend the goodness, wisdom, and love of God. It comes from two Greek words, *theos* and *dike*—God plus justice. Theodicy then is the human effort to justly defend God, so that in spite of all this rampant evil and runaway tragedy He still comes out the God of love the ancient Scriptures always claimed Him to be.

But is it possible to defend Him in the midst of our carnage?

Because, let's face it, human suffering comes in more shapes than just the shadowy form of death. In fact, death is not the ultimate suffering—death is the cessation of life, the end of suffering on this earth. When we weep, we do not weep for the one who died; we weep for the ones who survived! For it is the irony of human existence that suffering is greatest in life rather than in death.

In his classic book *Love Within Limits*, theologian Lewis Smedes defines suffering like this: "What all suffering really comes down to is the experience of anything we want very much not to experience" (p. 1).

So what is it you want very much not to experience? Getting fired from a job, getting flunked from your class? A bad date, a broken marriage, a bitter divorce? Bankruptcy? Mastectomy? Alzheimer's disease? The enfeeblement of old age? The list of our private fears is endless, isn't it? Add to these the colossal sufferings of war and famine and plagues globally, and the truth in any language or culture keeps getting spelled e-v-i-l.

Theodicy—defending a good God in an evil world. I have to confess that it gets harder and harder all the time in this world of escalating suffering, doesn't it?

But then again, maybe it never has been an easy proposition. Since the fall of Lucifer and Adam and Eve, "in the beginning," God has been faced with the global hemorrhaging of evil. But as we noted in chapter 4, God's response to evil was to willingly assume the blame and responsibility for human suffering, thus shifting the focus of His fledgling community of faith entirely to Him, until they were mature enough for a fuller exposé of evil's dark perpetrator. For that reason we find precious little in the Old Testament to deliver God from blame for the evils that befall us.

He was there

But there is one dusty little line from the heart of the Old Testament that offers a breathtaking portrait of God in the midst of our rampant suffering. A single line that pulls the drawstring on the veil of human suffering and opens for us a glimpse of God, a glimpse into His very thoughts in the midst of our very difficult lives. Isaiah saw it first, and I'm grateful he penned it for us to see too.

I like the way his line reads in the good old King James Version of the Bible: "In all their affliction he was afflicted" (Isaiah 63:9). If you look at the context of this verse, you discover that here Isaiah is reviewing the history of the Old Testament and a portion of the saga of suffering God's people have endured. Moving to the bottom line of Israel's saga and history, Isaiah draws us to a simple but profound reality: When they hurt, God hurt; when they suffered, God suffered; when they wept, God wept; when they were afflicted, God was afflicted.

What sort of mystery is this, this sort of strange, vicarious transferring of human suffering to the very heart of God?

It is the mystery of parenthood, is it not? As a father, I know a little of this mystery myself. Not so much how it works, but that it works. Our family was piling into the car once for a ride. My daughter Kristin was only about three years old at the time, and as I was getting things put into the car, I swung open the back door, and it stopped suddenly on its hinges with a dull thud. I spun around just in time to see her little hand shoot up to her forehead. I realized I had just swung the door straight into her head. It was another one of those slow motion moments when you're suspended in animation. Her mouth was open, sucking in huge drafts of what was about to rend the silence with a heartbreaking wail.

By the time she got her air, I had her in my arms. And I held her close, as my precious little girl sobbed out her unexpected pain and suffering. And I must tell you that as she cried out her pain, it was as if I could feel that pain too. I tell you the truth. I felt the pain, though the suffering was all hers. And her tears welled up in my eyes.

Truly, in her affliction I was afflicted. I can't explain how it works; I just know that it does. And so in a small measure I think I understand what God is saying when He announces through Isaiah "In all their affliction I was afflicted." It's the mystery of parenthood.

It's the mystery of God, who is transcendent in His power, but is ever present with me in my pain. In that classic on the life of Christ, *The Desire of Ages* by Ellen White, listen to this line: "Not a sigh is breathed, not a pain felt, not a grief pierces the soul, but the throb vibrates to the Father's heart" (p 356). In other words, in all of *our* afflictions, He is afflicted.

Why does it go on?

But there is yet another question we must face as we wrestle with this issue of theodicy. Maybe it occurred to you already. It's an obvious question, one that demands an answer: If God is so empathetic to our suffering and so powerful, why doesn't He just stop the suffering before it even starts? We can all understand how a feeble human father would accidentally open the car door onto his little girl. But where is omnipotent Father when our world comes crashing in? Why didn't He stop the pickup from hitting the car in the first place and stop the plane from crashing and stop the disease from spreading and stop the world from starving? Why would He choose to just suffer with us? Why not put an end to all the evil and pain? Why not just end the problem rather then continuing to endure the symptoms?

These are very fair questions to ask. And the answer has something to do with fairness too. Which is where the ancient story of Job enters, the great theodicy tale of Scripture. Job, the man who suffered so much, for whom life was truly very difficult.

Perhaps you know the story well already: One day God convenes a council in heaven, and apparently Satan is allowed to attend the council as the representative of this fallen planet. (He calls himself the prince of the world anyhow.) And seeing His rebel child Lucifer in attendance, God asks Satan, "Have you seen my friend Job? What a friend of Mine he is! Why there is no one more loyal to Me than Job!"

Satan looks back across the council at God upon His throne, and the rebel prince retorts, "Yes, Your Majesty, You're right. He's loyal all right. But let me tell You *why* he's loyal. It's because You have bribed him with your blessings. You've built a hedge around him, and Job feels very secure right now. But I guarantee You that if You pull the hedge away, Job will be the first to curse You to Your face! He may be a friend, but a fair-weather friend at best!"

The gauntlet has been thrown down. Lucifer challenges both God's fairness and freedom. Will Job still love God when the chips are not only down but gone? And so it is that God stares that devilish challenge to His fairness in the face and nods, "All right, you may touch Job. But spare his life."

Satan is gone. And true to his diabolical form, he soon unleashes a string of personal disasters upon Job that would send even the godliest of saints reeling. The devil strikes, and Job loses everything. He loses his property, his possessions, his children, and finally his health. He is a mere broken shell of his former self, squatting in the dust beneath the merciless sun, scraping the puss from his oozing sores with a shard of broken pottery. But Job does not turn on God. He remains a loyal friend. The record reads, "In all this Job did not sin or charge God with wrong-doing" (Job 1:22).

True freedom

This is the only place in the Old Testament where we catch a glimpse behind the veil of the human drama to witness the ferocity of the struggle between God and Satan—the fury of satanic rage against God and His creation, and the desperate struggle of God in the face of that withering attack to somehow win back the allegiance and loyalty of the rebel human race.

But through it all, it remains in the interest of fair play and freedom that God allows Satan to exercise his destructive power on this planet. Why? Because Satan has leveled his accusing finger at God, taunting that the only way God can get friends on this planet is to bribe them with blessings. "Take your blessings away, and they'll all come to me!" Satan says. And sad to say, to a large degree he's right—most of the world does turn to Satan.

What's at stake is the issue of human freedom and divine love. Does God love His people enough to let them be free to make their own choices? Because freedom is not true freedom unless it can be abused. Love is only love if it can be refused—if it can't be refused it isn't love. So by the very nature of love and freedom, God is compelled to allow love and freedom to unfold on earth through the choices made by human beings.

Lucifer and Adam and Eve were all given the freedom to choose. And it is their choices, and the billions of choices made by human beings since, that have created the hotbed of evil and sickbed of human misery we see on our planet today. We are all victims of these choices.

God's only hope is to somehow win our hearts back by His relentless love. To somehow get through to us with His message—that what Lucifer says isn't true. I am not a tyrant. I am not one who will bribe you to love me. I am your Father, your Friend. Come back to me.

But even when we do come back to Him we continue to suffer. We could understand it if the evil suffered and the righteous didn't. But even when we come back to God, we continue to suffer the effects of the evil in the world. So why doesn't God protect us?

Think about it for a moment. What would happen if, as soon as a person turned back to God, he or she were immunized—inoculated against evil and suffering? Would anybody ever want to go *home* to live with Him?   If we made a heaven out of this hell, who would want to leave it?

C. S. Lewis explained the situation on earth this way:

> The settled happiness and security which we all desire, God withholds from us by the very nature of the world: but joy, pleasure, and merriment He has scattered broadcast. . . . a few moments of happy love, a landscape, a symphony, a merry meeting with our friends, a bath or a football match. . . . Our Father refreshes us on the journey with some pleasant inns, but will not encourage us to mistake them for home (*The Problem of Pain*, 115).

The reality of human suffering continually reminds us of that old hymn that goes "This world is not my home,

I'm just a passin' through. . . . if heaven's not my home, then Lord what will I do. . . . the angels beckon me from heaven's open door, and I can't feel at home in this world anymore."

The prophets were right. We are aliens—strangers and pilgrims in search of a better world, citizens of the celestial kingdom. This is not home sweet home. As long as we live on this earth we will suffer the destructive fury of the dark enemy who claims the world and its inhabitants as his own, for we are living behind enemy lines.

There is no other way to understand all the tragedies we endure. Sure I've heard other explanations. Well-meaning people offer bromides such as, "Well, I'm sure God had a lesson in that tragedy for him." And I for one would never want to discount the human ability to learn from our suffering, but the fact remains that in too may cases the price is far too high for the lesson to be learned. Learning lessons isn't a satisfactory explanation for our pain and hurt.

Other well-meaning souls sometimes posit, "Perhaps then, God is trying to reach a loved one, a friend, a neighbor through that tragic death." And again, divine grace can triumph in the midst of any human tragedy and people have been "reached" through the suffering of others. But let us not transform God into a Being who at any instant could strike us down in hopes our demise would save another. How would you ever feel safe if you had to keep looking over your shoulder to see what God might be up to? Reaching others isn't a satisfactory explanation for human suffering either.

What reasons shall we give then for the bitterness of our suffering? As Richard Rice notes in his book *Why Bad Things Happen to God's People*, we may fall short of any reasons at all:

> On the universal, or cosmic, scale there is no justification for evil. And we cannot expect its consequences on the individual level always to make sense

either. Consequently, any response to suffering that looks back, that goes behind it to seek a specific reason in every instance, is bound to fail. And trying to explain the misfortunes that befall us usually just makes things worse (p. 26).

The fact is that while we have a need to be able to explain everything—to find a logical reason behind the tragedies that strike—there simply is no logic behind evil. Evil is the fruit of Lucifer's insanity. Period. Jesus was right all along, "An enemy has done this" (Matthew 13:28). The only plausible explanation for human suffering is that we still live behind enemy lines.

God weeps with us

And yet in the midst of our oftentimes irrational and inexplicable suffering comes the ringing assurance, "In all our afflictions, God is afflicted." For He is the God who suffers with His children. He may not say much to you right now. Maybe He only weeps with you. But there are times when words are too empty anyway.   In his book on suffering, Richard Rice tells the story of a professor he knew on the campus of the university where I am the pastor. It is a story that happened before my time here, but I know the family of the story.

A professor at the university was struck with a horrible, inexplicable tragedy. His young son was tragically killed in a playground accident on the ball field at school. The poor, grieving father and his family struggled to come to grips with their immense loss. People often wonder what they should say in the face of someone else's tragedy. But this father remembers the most comforting act anyone did for him during that time of intense pain and loss. One afternoon as the grieving father was in his university office a colleague, another professor, came to visit. He didn't speak a word. He just sat down that office of his friend. And he began to weep. He cried and cried. And then, without saying a word, he got up and left.

That grieving father later testified that his friend's being there, simply sharing the grief and tears for a time, meant more to him than any words could ever have said.

In your hour of suffering, God may be saying nothing to you at all, except "I'm crying with you."

In all our afflictions, He is afflicted! He holds our hand. And weeps.

But I remind you, the hand that holds yours is a nail-scarred hand. For He has already been to Calvary. And He has drunk the bitter dregs of the ultimate human pain. He is afflicted with us!

He went to Calvary so that all through eternity we would know: There is somebody who understands.

I love the way that Ellen White put this in the book *Education:*

> Few give thought to the suffering that sin has caused our Creator. All heaven suffered in Christ's agony; but that suffering did not begin or end with His manifestation in humanity. The cross is a revelation to our dull senses of the pain that, *from its very inception*, sin brought to the heart of God (263, emphasis added).

You see, there is another sufferer in this universe. His name is God. In all our afflictions, He too is afflicted. Because He's already been there, here. Which is why the ultimate word regarding ultimate suffering is that ultimately, intimately, God is with us.

And He will have the last word, when "He will wipe every tear from their eyes. There will be no more or mourning or crying or pain, for the old order of things has passed away " (Revelation 21:4, NIV). Heaven will be God's last word for the hell into which Lucifer has tried to turn this life.

At one of the two funerals I conducted for the young lives tragically snuffed out in that winter's plane crash, I stepped down from the pulpit at the end of the service to join the grieving family, who gathered about the open casket one last time and wept their tears over the stilled form of their son and grandson. In the presence of such anguished tears, what is there to say? A colleague and friend of mine for years, who had also been officiating at the service, stood beside me. We felt their tears in our own eyes and hearts.

After several minutes of silence, he leaned over to me and whispered the words that inspired the title of this chapter. "It's no wonder God can't sleep at night!"

Amid such tragedy, amid such human suffering, He neither slumbers nor sleeps, for in all our affliction He is afflicted.

What outrageous grace! What relentless love!

Chapter 9

Don't Worry,
Be Happy

You've no doubt heard the song that was the number one song of 1988 in America—garnering four prestigious Grammy awards the following year. It was a simple song that used no instruments, no accompaniments at all, except the singer's voice and his own whistling. And yet no other jingled tune has quite captured the fancy of the world in the same way! It shot its way up the solid gold charts, selling ten million copies in its first six months. Then it crossed over into the movie *Cocktail*, and that soundtrack sold more than eight million copies within a few months.

The catchy tune and snatchy lyrics were a global hit. Not that anybody had a choice, since the song's simple, repetitive message was drilled (or jingled) into the heads of men, women, and children all over the world over and over and over again. (Ad nauseam, some would later declare.)

A message so simple—simplistic may be a better adjective for it—that it didn't take long for its luster to grow dim! Though the record kept selling, as it kept preaching, "Don't worry, be happy!"

Or as composer and singer Bobby McFerrin kept singing: "Here's a little song I wrote, you might want to sing it note for note—Don't worry, be happy. . . .In every life we have some trouble, but when you worry you make it double—Don't worry, be happy. . . .When you worry, your face will frown, and that will bring everybody down—Don't worry, be happy!" Etc., etc.

Can you believe it? This nursery rhyme bit of quick-fix philosophy stole the show!

And is McFerrin happy? Apparently not. As with anything that gets a lot of media attention, soon there was a backlash, and even McFerrin himself grew tired of the song. According to an article in the February 1989 *Newsweek,* by that time he had decided never to perform the song in public again!

Let's face it—you can only sing a song like that so many times, you can only soothe your worried mind with platitudes for so long, before finally the truth breaks through. The truth that not worrying doesn't really solve anything. Sooner or later the truth breaks through in the sad realization that all the trite and inane platitudes in the world will never be able to slake our desperate thirst for lasting security and our insatiable hunger for genuine inner peace. "Don't worry, be happy" sounds great, but you can't just sing that song and expect all your troubles to go away, because they don't.

What we really want

You see surveys all the time of what it is that people really want, what it is that concerns them—what wakes them up in the middle of the night with a cold sweat. One survey I saw listed the top ten health concerns of Americans. What surprised me was not the first three items on the list—they were what you would expect in a health survey: Staying free from disease, avoiding smoking, and having an environment with clean air and clean water.

But the next items on the list seemed strangely out of

place. Do these seem like health concerns to you: Having someone to love, having a positive outlook on life, and having friends and family who are there for me when I need them.

They aren't what you'd expect from a survey of health concerns, but they certainly reveal what is on the minds of millions in our society. And for people with concerns like that, "Don't worry, be happy," just doesn't cut it. You can sing the words until you are blue in the face, but deep down inside your soul, there will still be a longing for something real, someone real, who will be there for you when the bottom of your life drops out.

When tragedy strikes, when we get ominous news, we want to be able to reach out and touch a real person who will respond with real concern. And I thank God for the compassionate and caring individuals you'll find in most every community, men and women whose big-heartedness is only a phone call away. People you and I can turn to when it seems there's no one else who cares. "Wounded healers," as Henri Nouwen once described them, people whose own life scars have empowered them to be the healing friends when we need them to. People who have more than "don't worry, be happy" with which to console us. Because there are times—too many times, really—when it is time to weep and not to smile, time to mourn and not to dance. Times when "grin and bear it" just won't cut it anymore.

The weeping prophet

Take the time of Jeremiah, for example. He has to be one of the saddest people to write in the Scriptures. They call him the weeping prophet. And not without reason, mind you. The poor man would have gone through Kleenex by the carton had he lived in our day. Teary-eyed and weepy-hearted. He's the author of the book of Jeremiah, and of another aptly titled book, Lamentations.

You might need to blow the dust off the pages when

you open your Bible to the book of Jeremiah. The fact is Christians don't tend to spend a lot of time in the Old Testament, and if your heart prefers to resonate with the song we've been talking about today, Jeremiah probably isn't one of your favorite books, because in it there is a lot of sadness, a lot of worry.

For several chapters now we've been looking at what I call "a tale of two mountains." We've briefly relived the events at Mount Sinai—and the spectacular theophany in which God personally gave the Ten Commandments amidst exploding fire, thunder, and earthquake. We've also been pondering what happened on another mountain top, Mount Calvary (or Mount Golgotha) centuries later. Two summits in our quest to know the God who appeared at the top of them both.

Jeremiah, historically speaking, and perhaps philosophically speaking, is a man caught dead center between those two mountains. He's caught in the crossfire, as it were. Which is why we find him crying so much of the time.

But what would you expect of a man who is living all the time with the headlines of heartache? Jeremiah lived in treacherous times. He lived in a kingdom that was going through its death throes. The army of Babylon, the enemy, was literally camped on the doorstep. Refugees from all over the land of Judah were streaming into Jerusalem, bereaved, beleaguered, and seemingly forsaken by their God, telling tales of terror and carnage too horrible for consolation. It was no time for him to be singing "Don't worry, be happy!"

And that is what makes the message of Jeremiah 31:3, 4 seem so strange, so incongruous, so out of place. Take a look for yourself: "The LORD appeared to us in the past, saying: 'I have loved you with an everlasting love; I have drawn you with loving-kindness. I will build you up again and you will be rebuilt, O Virgin Israel. Again you will take up your tambourines and go out to dance with the joyful' " (NIV).

In the preceding chapter Jeremiah has been warning the people of disaster, judgment, and destruction to come, and then suddenly he breaks forth with this song of unfettered love and joy from the Father. It almost seems too good to be true, doesn't it? It almost seems like God Himself is saying "Don't worry, be happy!"

Believe me, we all could use a joy experience like that from time to time, couldn't we? I'll be the first to admit that I personally would benefit from a chance to simply let all my worries go, to pick up a tambourine and dance— not the sensual slither and gyrating that passes for dance today, but the light-hearted, joy-filled movement that radiates a joy in the Lord, when the heart throbs with happiness, and the head is thrown back and we shout with unbridled gladness!

That's what God is promising here, and that is what we all could use more of, when life's cares weigh us down so heavily.

The only problem is we may not be so sure what there is to even dance about! What shall set our hearts to singing?

Everlasting love

Jeremiah finds a reason for joy in this message from God: " 'I have loved you with an everlasting love; I have drawn you with loving-kindness' " (31:3 NIV). And that's certainly something worth dancing about! *Everlasting* love! What a concept! Especially in our day, when we know so little of lasting love.

This is not just romantic love. You know how that goes. Johnny gazes deeply into Sherri's alluring eyes, and whispers the words "I'll love you for ever!"

The only trouble is, that three months ago he was saying the same thing to Kari, and three months from now he'll probably be saying it to Terri. And sometime later, he'll be marrying Mary!

We don't know the meaning of everlasting love. Even in marriage, love often doesn't last. What does it mean to love someone in this way: " 'I have loved you with an everlasting love; I have drawn you with loving-kindness. I will build you up again and you will be rebuilt, O Virgin Israel. Again you will take up your tambourines and go out to dance with the joyful' " (Jeremiah 31:3, 4)?

Do you know what everlasting love means in this context? In the book of Jeremiah? Remember the history. All hell is about to break loose upon the people of Jerusalem. The enemy, Nebuchadnezzar, has already hit the city twice. One more strike and they'll be out for good! Shattered, broken, and gone. It makes you wonder doesn't it, how under heaven God can be speaking of everlasting love and dancing with tambourines on the eve of such destruction!

The only way this promise from God can make any sense at all, the only way I can fathom His apparent "Don't worry, be happy" rejoinder to their impending doom, is the conclusion that even when I am totally down and out, God apparently is not! No matter how bad things may be or get for me, no matter what private hell you may be going through right now, the very simple message here is that God's love is *everlasting*. Which being interpreted means that even when I feel like quitting, God doesn't!

We may quit loving Him, but He won't quit loving us. We may quit trusting, but He won't quit believing in us. He keeps on loving and believing and giving to us . Which, Jeremiah reminds us, is reason enough for us not to pawn off our tambourines yet or sell off our dancing shoes. For "again you will take up your tambourines and go out to dance with the joyful."

Sadly, there are too many people who haven't heard this bit of good news. The latest statistics from the United States Centers for Disease Control indicate that more people die from suicide every day than from homicide. We worry so about the crime rate, and the chance of being killed by someone else, but in reality, we are too often our own worst enemies. More people kill themselves than are killed by others. They just give up all hope for the future and end it all. The statistics are particularly alarming when you look at teen and child suicide. Between 1952 and 1992 the incidence of suicide among adolescents and young adults nearly tripled. Between 1980 and 1992 the rate of suicide among those aged 10 to 14 more than doubled, going up by 120%! Every 24 hours thirteen Americans between the ages of 15 and 24 commit suicide. The attempts at self-destruction are much higher—one statistic I read indicated that a teenager attempts suicide once every seventy-eight seconds in the United States!

"Don't worry, be happy." But in spite of the jingle, there are so many brokenhearted, broken-hoped people in the world. So many quitters!

Before we judge any of them too quickly or harshly, let's admit what we all know too well—we're all quitters. Be honest. We know very little of everlasting commitment. We quit our jobs, we quit school, we quit our friends, we give up and quit on our marriages, we quit on our kids, we quit on ourselves, on our once-upon-a-time dreams. We quit singing, we quit dancing, we quit trying, we quit living. We quit.

Maybe it's your heart that is planning on quitting today, tonight, right now. Maybe you've all but given up. But, friend, before you do, take one more look at the heart of God.

Consider God's heart

After all, nobody could more down and out than Israel was when Jeremiah penned these words. The besieged, defeated people were ready to throw in the tattered towel and call it quits. Forever. And then it was that above the din and doom of their plight God spoke: I will *never* quit! I will *never quit loving you*! *Forever*!

" 'I have loved you with an everlasting love; I have

drawn you with loving-kindness.' "

To a people who had wasted their lives and blown their chances, God promises His *everlasting* love. Forever.

That is what He was *dying* to tell us on the rocky summit of the second mountain, Golgotha. When Jesus stretched out His arms, and they nailed Him to that bloody cross, He knew that now at last He could tell the whole truth about God.

Did you catch the simple prayer of His dying breath? " 'Father, forgive them, for they do not know what they are doing' " (Luke 23:34). The portrait of God never shined more brightly than in that death prayer!

For when Jesus prayed that prayer, He was revealing to us the ultimate truth any human can ever learn about God: God is by nature a relentless Lover and an unconditional Forgiver. It is not only second nature to Him, it is His first nature, too!

Some would paint a harsh, stern picture of God, claiming that He needed the cross to turn Him from condemner to forgiver, but the shining portrait of Calvary's death prayer is not of One who needed to climb the hill to *become* a forgiver. He climbed it *because* He was a forgiver.

God didn't need Calvary to change His mind about us.

He needed Calvary to change our minds about Him!

"I have *always* loved you with an everlasting love," He says to us.

Relentless love! Unconditional forgiveness!

Please note carefully that on that fateful Friday (now *Good* Friday) there was not a single soul atop that mountain that was asking to be forgiven, save for a dying thief at the end of the day. But of the "them" that Jesus breathes His prayer for, not a single one of them was praying for forgiveness. Cursing and jeering the Forgiver, yes. Begging His forgiveness, never!

When Jesus looks down from that bloody perch, His tortured gaze finds no human heart, not one who is begging to be forgiven. But Jesus looks down on that unrepentant, hateful mob, and prays that prayer anyhow: "Father, please! It doesn't matter. Forgive all of them. They don't know what they're doing!"

Whether you ask for it or not, God—because He is by nature a relentless Lover and an unconditional Forgiver— offers you forgiveness. Period.

Dealing with sin

Do you realize what that means? When you fail and fall and your sin is splattered all over your heart and you are overwhelmed with your own guilt . . . when you've already confessed that sin a thousand times before . . . when your tortured conscience taunts you into giving up and quitting on God . . . don't. Instead, remember the truth: God is by nature—He cannot be otherwise and be Himself—a lover and forgiver. In your guilty grief throw yourself into His outstretched arms and wide-open embrace.

If only it would spring to mind, the moment we fall in sin—My Father is a forgiver by nature, I can this instant go home to Him, and His arms will be outstretched, for He has already forgiven me! Oh, how much heartache and grief and guilt could be spared were we to believe and behave this truth! Gone the ominous cloud that keeps crushing us down with a sense of defeated failure and hopeless despair.

Now, look, this is not a plea for continued sinning. It is a promise for the contrite sinner. Nobody, least of all God, is calling for some sort of let's-make-a-deal kind of bargaining here. As long as I keep saying I'm sorry, I can keep on sinning. Hardly!

But Jeremiah's promise and Jesus' prayer are both crimson clear that God is a lover and forgiver by nature, not by negotiation. Of course, I must confess my sin to Him. Not because He has to be persuaded, but because I need to reminded that Calvary was the price for *my* sin and the place for *His* love.

Everlasting love.

"'I have loved you with an everlasting love; I have drawn you with loving-kindness. I will build you up again and you will be rebuilt. . . . Again you will take up your tambourines and go out to dance with the joyful.'"

Don't worry—when you come to Me—be happy!

When you hear God speaking those words, it is no wonder the heart feels like dancing! For on an old summit, we have found a new song in God's heart.

It is the song of relentless love. And outrageous grace.

A song you, too, can sing and share.

Forever.